THE
IAN
HEALY
STORY

PLAYING
FOR
KEEPS

*I dedicate this book to the
Healy and the Perkins families
for the eternal support of
myself and my wife when
I am on tour.*

"BALLAD OF A BATTLER"

There's a man who must be honoured
For the trouper that he's been
A bloke who knows the spirit
Of the sacred baggy green
A larrikin who battles
For the country that he loves
A cheeky little bastard
With a golden pair of gloves.
Crouching for a victim
In the shadow of the stumps
There is Aussie in his ticker
And the claret that it pumps.
He greets the pacing batsmen
With a friendly little sledge
Then shows him where the shed is
After pouncing on his edge.
And when that lump of willow
Comes to be in his possession
No matter what the score is
He will wield it with aggression.
The scorer's always busy
When his blazing bat is served
His hundred at Old Trafford
Was a hundred well deserved.
Whenever next you're at the pub
And beer is what appeals
Raise your glass, salute your flag
And drink a toast to Heals.

JASON 'RUPERT' McCALL

THE
IAN HEALY
STORY

An Autobiography

PLAYING
FOR
KEEPS

As told to Robert Craddock

SWAN
PUBLISHING

ACKNOWLEDGEMENTS

Heals would like to thank the following people for their
help in the compilation of this book.

Nev, Rae, Ken, Greg, and Helen Healy, Kim Boon, Brad Inwood,
Mark Templeton, Grant O'Hara, Dave Lyle, Adrian McGregor,
Ian Perkins, Jim Tucker, Kate Applegarth, Roseanna Neser, Steve Waugh,
Trevor Barsby, Merv Hughes, Mike Blucher, Perry Mason, Merv Bidgood,
Chris White, Rupert McCall and the late Charlee Marshall.

Ian Healy also gratefully acknowledges the following people
and organisations for their generous assistance in providing
the photographs for *Playing For Keeps*.

Gregg Porteous, Trent Parke, Ray Titus, Viv Jenkins, Steve Waugh,
Graham Morris, Simon Renilson, Peter Cronin, News Ltd,
The Courier-Mail/ Brisbane, Australian Cricket Board,
Australian Picture Library/All Sport, *Inside Edge*/PBL Marketing.

Some photos in this book are from Ian Healy's personal collection;
they have been kindly provided to Ian Healy by cricket
photographers from around the world, and include
Graham Morris, Phillip Brown, A Laing and Bruce Postle.

Ian Healy also gratefully acknowledges
AUSTRALIA POST, CHANNEL NINE and CARLTON & UNITED BREWERIES
for their generous support.

First published in 1996 by
Swan Publishing Pty Ltd
Suite 14C, 81 Waratah Ave. Dalkeith, W.A. 6009

Copyright © 1996
Swan Publishing Ltd

National Library of Australia
Cataloguing-in-Publication data

Craddock, Robert, 1961- .
The Ian Healy story : playing for keeps.

ISBN 0 9586760 0 3.

1. Healy, Ian. 2. Cricket players - Australia - Biography
3. Cricket - Wicket-keeping. I. Title.

796.358092

Printed in Australia by McPherson's Printing Group

Designer: Stan Lamond, Lamond Art & Design

CONTENTS

FOREWORD

Over the years Australia has been blessed with a string of excellent glovemen, among them Don Tallon and Wally Grout, Rod Marsh and now Ian Healy. So often the unsung heroes (as 'Heals' often calls himself, "just the drummer in the band") wicket-keepers are vital to the team's success, for they are the heartbeat of the side, the ones from whom inspiration is sought and the ones who set the standards for the rest of the players to live up to.

Heals does all of the above and plenty more and that is why he is so highly regarded by not only his fellow players, but opponents and spectators alike.

I first heard the name "Healy" when he was the bolt from the blue selection in the Australian team to Pakistan in 1988, and like most others I didn't know much about him at all.

That was soon to change, for his character is such that he became a popular and well-liked member virtually from day one of that tour.

His initial Test appearance was probably best described as "ordinary" (like that of the rest of the team in that game). However, he did take a superb diving catch early in the match that led the boys to think the selectors had pulled a masterstroke by picking this unknown lad who hailed from the small Queensland town of Biloela.

From this first Test Heals would have to be one of the few cricketers I've ever seen who continues to improve and expand his skills with each passing match. He sets a standard that appears to be the ultimate in one game, only to surpass it in his next outing; that is why he will continue to set records that will be the benchmark for future 'keeper-batsmen to strive for.

Enough about his obvious talents. I'm sure people would like to know a bit about his habits, trademarks, quirks, likes and dislikes, which make him a much valued and unique team member. After rooming with Heals a few times I am continually amazed, dumbfounded, shocked and in awe of a man who can get up in the early hours of a morning before practice or a game, put on his inner gloves and take a golf ball down to the basement of a hotel or its carpark and repeatedly bounce this little white object off, at all angles, in order to get his glovework and footwork techniques right for the upcoming game. That to me is what you call dedication.

If there's ever been a neater cricketer to pull on the boots I've yet to hear or see of him. Heals is fanatical about his appearance, with each item of clothing folded immaculately in its designated space in the locker, wristbands evenly placed on the arms, pads free of dirt and abrasions, gloves glistening from his regular maintenance and polishing, and shoes as clean and white as freshly fallen snow. It's enough to make one feel ashamed, especially if you're sitting next to 'the immaculate one' in the change rooms. This is what you call having pride in yourself and who you're representing.

We've shared so many memorable moments together during our careers. We were at the crease together when Heals scored his first Test century at Old Trafford, I've shared a beer with Heals as he shed a tear in an English Embassy in Lahore when he thought he cost Australia Test victory, we've worn the baggy green cap to the celebration party in Jamaica, well into the early hours after claiming the Frank Worrell Trophy. I've seen him in agony on the team physio bench with an ice pack on his groin after taking three blows in succession against the might of the West Indies quicks and I've shared a cigar when his first child was born while we were away on tour overseas.

Heals is a man who enjoys a beer with his mates, doesn't mind a spot of McDonald's in his diet, rates himself highly in the fashion stakes, couldn't grow a beard if his life depended on it, and enjoys running on treadmills, to name a few of his lesser known quirks. He is also a great motivator, whether it be on or off the field. He has led many times by selflessly sacrificing his wicket in the quest for a team win, played under duress due to injury and guided the team in joyous celebrations in his new role as team leader of "Under the Southern Cross I stand", the team song.

All of these qualities make him a person who the average Australian can identify with and be proud of, and they are also why he is always one of the first players to be picked in any side and a guy you would want by your side in troubled times. Australian cricket is lucky to have him.

STEVE WAUGH

The two of us playing it cool in the Caribbean cricketing cauldron in 1991.

GREGG PORTEOUS/NEWS LTD

THE BEST VIEW IN THE HOUSE

*"Keeping wickets is for the adventurous,
those who bore easily and, on reflection, those
with just a touch of stupidity."*

ROD MARSH

They say you never forget your first schoolboy romance, but I have another especially vivid memory of my youth—the day I began a glove affair that would dictate the course of my life.

It was just another unspectacular bush training session, no different from thousands of others, yet the memory of it sits in my mind as clearly as my first Test match.

I was at the Biloela High School oval where we were trialling for the Callide-Dawson Under-11 team. I was only nine at the time and I watched with interest as a 10-year-old boy was groomed in the art of 'keeping.

The amount of work he was getting just seemed to appeal to me and from that point I wanted to be a wicket-keeper.

There is a special bond between 'keepers only we can truly understand. Much to the fascination of some team-mates, I spend a lot of time talking to my opposite number, no matter who it is.

Sometimes a team-mate such as Mark Taylor will walk into an opposition dressing room and see me seated beside my rival 'keeper and remark, "Have a look at these two dumbos."

He will then follow it up with something cerebral like, "You don't see me pairing off with their opening batsman." And I will fire back with, "Well maybe if you did you might learn something."

Unless you have been a 'keeper it's difficult to understand the 'keeper's lot. In your entire career you might speak to 10 people who fully understand the job. We love talking shop ... what sort of gloves we use, what type of work we are doing, what problems we are having and why we are having them.

The camaraderie enjoyed by 'keepers was evident at the Singer tournament in Sri Lanka in 1994. Indian 'keeper Nayan Mongia organised a dinner with Pakistani gloveman Rashid Latif and myself, and I learnt something quite curious about the world of cricket. Latif told me he had seen every Test I had played in Australia. He had watched them on Star television, which beams Test series from throughout the world to the subcontinent.

It struck me then that the Indians and Pakistanis knew much more about us than we knew about them.

I am particularly close to England's Jack Russell; if Jack is talking to an Australian journalist he will say, "Tell Healy I will be part of the 1997 Ashes campaign ... just make sure he is as well."

Jack is an artist of some repute and I told him I'd like one of his paintings to hang up in my new house. Soon after, a batch of high quality prints arrived from overseas.

Jack eats Wheetbix with honey in the dressing room during a day and also has honey with tea at the drinks break, a favoured refreshment of Alan Knott.

Wicket-keepers can be an eccentric bunch. 'Knotty' once saw me walking naked through a dressing room at Old Trafford in 1989 during a tea break and was quite amazed ... not by my physical dimensions, but by the fact that I could get undressed and dressed again in a 20 minute break.

*A character of the game, a fine artist, a top class gloveman
and a good mate is England's Jack Russell.*

He said he couldn't do it and I can understand why, because he used to wear more gear than a mannequin at an army disposal shop ... a singlet, several hankies and bibs as well as the traditional items such as a shirt, pants, and pads etc.

'Keepers are the best judges of 'keepers. A compliment or a criticism from another 'keeper means a lot to me. In 1989 I sat down with the West Indies legend, the elastic, athletic rubber man Jeff Dujon. He told me that my work was too hard and that I should relax and be much softer in every aspect of the game, my footwork, my gloving of the ball, everything.

I delight in the quaint traditions of our craft. When I first played for Australia another former Test 'keeper, Brisbane's John Maclean took me to lunch. He said Wally Grout had done the same for him earlier in his career and I plan to do the same for the player who takes the batten from me at State or national level.

Maclean, with Rod 'Bacchus' Marsh, was a boyhood idol of mine. When I was 11 Maclean came to Biloela, my home town, with the Queensland side and Mum took me along to meet him and get some advice on gloves. My first set of gloves were John Maclean autographs.

As a child I formed an opinion that Marsh and Maclean were the embodiment of everything a wicket-keeper should be. They were always in the thick of things, hustling, urging, keeping the blokes pepped up and never out of the front line. I just couldn't imagine a team with a quiet wicket-keeper; they do at times seem like a band without a conductor.

Sometimes even the 'keeper needs a bit of spice in proceedings to pep him up. I could sense my motivation slipping during a drawn out day in the field against Orange Free State on the 1993–94 South African tour when a portly batsman called Kosie Venter came to the crease.

He was one of those blokes who just looked like a character and he brought out the larrikin in me.

I kept on calling things to the bowler like, "C'mon Shane, we'll put a Mars bar just short of a length and get this bloke stumped."

Kosie turned around and said, "I'd have to be pretty quick to beat Boonie from short leg." The whole exchange lifted me and made me concentrate more easily.

After admiring Marsh's work for so long it was quite a moment for me to meet him. It came during my first international summer when we had a Saturday off during the Perth one-dayers and I ventured up to him in the commentary area.

He was slightly withdrawn and I could see that just because I was the current Test match custodian didn't automatically mean Marsh rated me highly. I had to earn my spurs before he would take me on board.

Our first meeting overwhelmed me. My mind spun. He talked in fairly

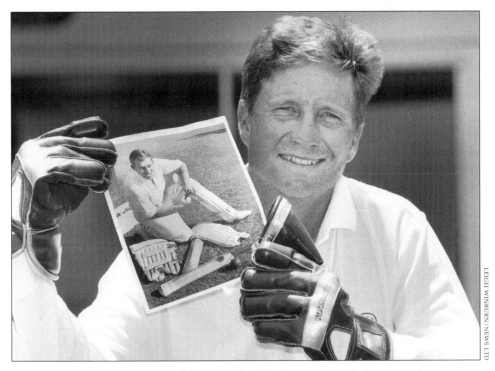

*Queensland has a proud heritage of wicket-keepers, one of whom was the
late Wally Grout, one of Australia's finest, and a character to boot.*

general terms with advice like, "When you are batting belt anything that's
up and get out of the road of anything in their half."

He made it all sound so easy but my mind was ticking over at a million
miles per hour.

It was not until the following season, after the 1989 Ashes triumph, that I
could sense him warming to me. We had a training session at a local park in
Perth and it turned out to be essential to my long-term development. He
showed me how to move my feet better and took me through other routines
which were so impressive I was able to convince coach Bob Simpson to follow Marsh's methods at training.

Marsh, who previously had supported Western Australia's Tim 'Ziggy'
Zoehrer strongly in the media, asked me how Ziggy went on the 1989 Ashes
tour and I told him my honest opinion ... he stuffed up by not practising
enough. I sensed Marsh had heard other similar feedback and decided that
I might be around for some time and that he would help me.

As incongruous as it sounds, it took a verbal roasting for me to feel that I
had finally arrived at Test level ... at least in Marsh's discerning eyes. It was
some months later, and followed a victorious day-night game in Melbourne.
I was enjoying a beer at the Hilton and Rod came over with a king bee in
his bonnet.

He said, "Listen mate, if you are not going to take my advice and listen to what I say I won't even bother talking to you in future."

A dumbfounded "What?" was the best I could do for a reply.

He said, "I saw the way you were practising today and 'Simmo' was hitting catches willy nilly. You were getting very lazy."

So I took that on board and from that point have always trained the way Marsh trained, which is the way I liked. From then on I knew 'Bacchus' was with me, because he had spent the energy in chastising me, which meant he saw something worthwhile and was looking after me. Now I can easily approach him.

When I was first chosen for Australia one journalist led his story with the words, "Australia is still to convince itself it has a 'keeper worthy of following the great Rod Marsh."

That may have been true and I was certainly feeling a multitude of pressures. But six 'keepers had been chosen between Rod and myself; the yardstick for me at that time was not so much Rod's record but those of the men who had followed him.

I admired Queensland predecessor Peter Anderson for his attention to detail, but that did not mean I agreed with every facet of his play. I was always a disciple of the Australian way of 'keeping fashioned by Marsh, which dictated that a 'keeper should move his feet quickly, never dive unless he had to, and always attempt to take the ball on the inside of his body.

Ando was a staunch admirer of the Alan Knott and Bob Taylor school of glovemanship, and 'kept like an English 'keeper, in that he moved with straighter legs, took the ball in front of his body and would dive further.

Like Marsh and Maclean, I always wanted to stay on my feet where possible—Mum vigorously encouraged me to do so for the practical purpose of stopping me from getting dirty! When I first started 'keeping I had no idea what a good game with the gloves was, but I have become more goal orientated.

Over the last 30 or so Tests I have looked at Rod Marsh on the distant mountain top of 355 dismissals in 96 Tests and realised that averaged out to about 3.6 dismissals per Test. That has become a quiet goal for me. Presently I have 275 victims from 79 matches. If I had used Rod's career as a motivational carrot earlier in my own career, I could have drawn more out of myself. It would have lifted my enthusiasm and attitude, particularly in dull games.

If I match Marsh's achievements in similar time it will prove to me that there were some unsung performers in my era and that the likes of Hughes and McDermott deserve to be a union to join Lillee and Thomson in Australian cricket's Hall of Fame.

For many years I felt the fastest bowler I had 'kept to was that of Merv

Hughes during his quickest years of 1988–89, though Craig McDermott at times drew close.

But Glenn McGrath's work on the 1995 West Indian tour was comparable to Merv at his quickest.

This may surprise some, but Merv would always look faster than McGrath because of his hostile demeanour and assaults on the batsmen's bodies. Glenn was smoother and pitched the ball up more, so he never looked as sharp, but he was comfortably as quick as any of the West Indies in our memorable series win in '95.

Merv was always among the most difficult bowlers to 'keep to, not only because of his sheer speed but because the ball would often wobble in the air after passing the batsman. I was always on edge when he was bowling.

Another supreme challenge is 'keeping to Shane Warne. On a fifth day wicket it is a handful for the batsmen, so you can imagine how much harder it is for me with my view blocked by the man at the crease.

I have never 'kept to Wasim Akram, but I rate him a potential nightmare. One of the reasons Pakistan cannot settle on a 'keeper is because he is so difficult to 'keep to.

With clever changes of pace, the ability to swing the ball late, both ways at searing pace Akram can regularly wrong foot a 'keeper. The tendency is to follow the initial line of the ball, but the late movement and then the edge that often follows it means a 'keeper must have good hands and sharp reflexes to survive.

To make Akram more of a challenge, he does much of his work on the slow subcontinent wickets where you must stand closer to avoid catching the ball at ankle height, but every now and then you get a flyer. Speaking as a batsman, he is the quickest I've faced, the only bowler from whom I've hit a ball that I didn't actually see. It happened twice in a Test match in Melbourne.

Don't ask me how I got a bat on the ball both times; it is probably just a matter of reflexes, honed by hundreds of hours of practice, clicking onto automatic pilot.

I like listening to or reading about old 'keepers, because our craft hasn't changed much over the years.

Greg Chappell's grandfather Victor Richardson told him that no matter how clever you think you are in inventing something, don't get too carried away because the chances are someone has used it before. There are times when I believe he is spot-on. Someone sent me a copy of a 1934 edition of Brisbane's *The Courier-Mail* where then-Test 'keeper Bertie Oldfield was explaining how to take a bumper over the stumps.

The advice was word perfect to that you would give today.

Australia has always been proud of its 'keeping heritage, and the man who is continually touted as this nation's greatest is Bundaberg's Don Tallon. No lesser judges than Sir Donald Bradman and Bill Brown rate Tallon the best they have seen.

Tallon, who, in photos I have seen, had the sun-dried look of a hardy old Queenslander, 'kept for the Maroons for 20 years and it was said his hands were so soft he could have been a violinist after he retired, so little damage had he sustained to his tools of trade.

You hear fascinating tales about glovemen such as Australia's turn-of-the-century custodian Jack Blackham 'keeping over the stumps to some rampaging fast bowlers.

There are times when I wonder how fast the great pacemen of yesteryear really were ... I would love to go back in time.

During the 1993 Ashes tour I was gazing at a clubhouse photo of former Lancashire and Australian fast bowler of the 1920s, Ted McDonald, when a local fan said, "That man was supposed to be one of the fastest bowlers of all time ... as quick as anything we've seen."

The photo had Ted delivering the ball from one end but, significantly, at the other end the 'keeper and slips were standing only five metres behind the stumps.

Ted may have been fast for his era—and that is all that matters—but it would be folly to compare his pace with Jeff Thomson in his prime, when no 'keeper or slips cordon stood closer than 20 metres to the bat.

Even Australia's long-serving coach Bob Simpson does not fully appreciate the nuances of the craft, and team-mates have no idea either. And I can understand why. When 'Tubby' Taylor took the gloves off me in South Africa and I stood at first slip I reckoned what he was doing looked easy, yet I was mentally battling my backside off for most of the day doing the same job.

I know bowlers don't fully appreciate the concentration required because I often get asked by them, "Could you just watch my front arm in the delivery stride and tell me if everything is where it should be?" That's like asking a matador if he could spare a few cursory seconds to check the brand on a bull as it charges him. They have no idea that I am supposed to be watching the ball and by watching it I mean watching it separately from the bowler's hand and all the way through its flight path.

So if your team-mates don't understand the job, what chance the media who influence the public? A 'keeper must accept he is the no-frills middle man, the nuts and bolts operator ... just a drummer in the band.

Recently I read some ageless advice from Oldfield, who said it was important for a 'keeper to showcase his skills. He said, "If you get the chance make sure you let people know what goes into your skills. If you make a good leg-side stumping don't just dismiss it as routine. Tell them how you practise for it and how you couldn't sight the ball behind the batsman's body and had to snap into action very quickly to pick his pocket before he had his foot down. Tell them how hard it is."

That struck a chord with me because my style is an undemonstrative one and it made me think that it is worthwhile making your skills more evident. It can't do wicket-keeping any harm.

Being good enough to play for Australia is one thing, getting there quite another and, as I know better than anyone, a matter of fickle circumstance.

Sometimes when I have practised with my Queensland understudies, Wade Seccombe and Gavin Fitness (now in South Australia), I wonder, Why am I 'keeping for Australia and they are not?

What sets us apart? Is it ability or simply opportunity? As we practise in front of the Queensland Cricketer's Club I often think that patrons sharing a drink on the balcony must watch me take 50 catches, then Gavin and Wade take the same, and conclude there is nothing between us.

Quite often the difference may only be a hairline and it might just come down to who prepares better.

Spectators might think our catching looks robotic but all the while I am trying to program my mind, to get speed in my footwork, to take the ball on the inside of my body. I will visualise a right-handed batsman missing the ball, then a left-handed batsman and various other things in a hope to condition my subconscious to every possible match-day eventuality. If you simply stand there and catch, it won't do you much good at all.

Some players just can't wait to have a try at wicket-keeping. During the World Cup South Africa's Jonty Rhodes made Warnie break up when he impersonated Garry Kirsten 'keeping to left-arm spinner Paul Adams after Dave Richardson was injured.

He said Kirsten, who had trouble reading Adams, would try and cover both sides of the stumps by going one way with his gloves and tossing his leg out the other side in case the ball spun the other way.

New Zealand captain Martin Crowe was another who fancied himself behind the stumps.

Kiwi 'keeper Ian Smith tells the story of Crowie taking the gloves in a Test against the West Indies when the Windies needed 30 runs in their second innings for victory.

To liven up a low key session the Kiwis made a collective effort to ensure that under no circumstances was the ball to touch Martin's gloves.

They even briefed openers Gordon Greenidge and Desmond Haynes, who were most amused and consequently played extravagant defensive pushes at wide balls they would have normally left alone to make sure Martin didn't touch the ball.

Crowie became increasingly frustrated and would yell "'*Keeper*" with great emotion every time a ball was pushed to a fieldsman. But the clued-up Kiwi fieldsmen would spin on their heels and toss the ball to the bowler.

Crowe couldn't believe the way the ball was going to everyone except him. But he sensed a gee-up when, upon leaving the field, he was slapped on the back by team-mates who said, "Well 'kept."

There have been times when I felt the 'keeper's contribution was sold short. During the 1994–95 summer in a one-day match against Zimbabwe in Perth I had a sound day behind the stumps and then scored an important 40 as we scored 8–167 in reply to Zimbabwe's 9–166.

Yet Shane Warne won man-of-the-match for his 2–27. Feeling a bit neglected, I said, "If that's not a Channel Nine decision I don't know what is."

I was spotlighting Warnie's connections with Channel Nine (who now employ me) and he was most upset about it. We had it out over the next few days and he said to me, "You just can't say that, Heals, it's bullshit."

It was basically just the 'keeper coming out in me.

There have also been times I've received more credit than I deserved. Once against Zimbabwe in Hobart the commentators raved about a leg-side signal I had given Tim May, which resulted in Andy Flower tickling one behind his pads into my gloves.

What actually happened was Flower, in tapping his bat at the crease, flicked a bit of turf back towards me. He apologised, but I told him not to worry and I tossed it away with my right glove.

Maysie saw my glove movement and took this to mean a signal, so he bowled it down the leg side and I pouched an edge, whipped off the bails and both umpires raised their fingers.

Broken bones and general joint injuries are just a fact of life in this job. My left index finger does not bend in the middle joint, both little fingers have lost 10 degrees when I attempt to straighten them and my right index finger is a bit bulbous.

I cannot come to terms with the fact that a sore finger can cost you a Test match, so I have tried to live with such setbacks. If you have a ligament strain or a broken finger the standard rehabilitation process is to have it in a splint for six weeks, which is just unacceptable from my professional viewpoint. Add a couple of weeks for regaining match practice and that means you could be out of the summer for two months for a sore finger ... it's just not on.

I know I can play with pain and not let the team down, but there have been moments of distress and self-doubt along the way.

I broke my left index finger in two places on the last day of the last Test against England in Perth in 1990–91 taking a leg-side catch off Mike Atherton, and when I came off the field it was as black as a looming thunder cloud.

I had X-rays when I returned to Brisbane and Dr John McKnee told me I shouldn't take part in the West Indies tour, which was leaving in a week.

But I responded with, "Sorry, I'm going," and, after keeping a copy of my

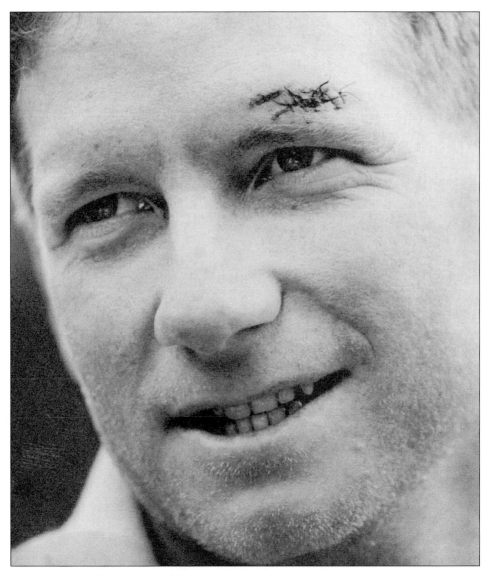

Six stitches is the message in this photo—six in my eyebrow,
because the six in the ball hit me!

X-rays for some lectures he was doing, he referred me to Dr Peter Myers, who said, "I can't stop you from going ... good luck."

It was important for me to strengthen my relationship with Myers if I were to get through the tour. I wanted to prove to him that I knew what I was capable of and wasn't just trying to be a cavalier fool.

But it was the most pain I had ever suffered and certainly the most long-lasting. I couldn't hold a bat properly at my first net session, which was almost comically inept.

The bat was spinning in my hand and the ball was barely running into the side net. I made a duck in the First Test in Jamaica, but fortunately rallied to contribute 53 and 47 in the Second Test in Georgetown.

Hand injuries are such a curse for wicket-keepers I can still recall the joyous moment when I realised the injury had been left behind. It was at Barbados six weeks later, when a return rocketed in from the boundary in front of the dressing rooms. I took it and, to my amazement and immense relief, didn't feel a thing ... the nightmare was over.

Several years later when I broke my thumb in Pakistan and had to miss the last Test of the tour, I went to Myers again and we cut every corner to ensure I was available for the First Test against England.

I had a five week deadline, so we pushed every recovery process to the limit, taking the plaster off in eight days instead of 13 in order to ensure I got to the line.

Every 'keeper has his favourite dismissals and two stand out for me. The first was a diving one-handed leg-side interception of stubborn Sri Lankan Ravi Ratnayake in Hobart in 1990.

I had been chastened by a line in the pen pictures of a cricket program which had called me "a dependable type who mightn't let you down but would never win you a match".

The Sri Lankans, particularly Ravi, had been providing stubborn resistance on the last day of the Test, but I dived full length to my right to haul in a leg-side tickle off Ratnayake, which changed the match.

But perhaps my favourite catch was from Ken Rutherford's defensive blade in New Zealand to a ball from Shane Warne that turned as if it had hit Tony Greig's car keys.

It pitched almost a metre outside leg stump and screwed across Rutherford's body, just clipping bat on the way, which made it go further.

I followed it all the way with my gloves and, given the freakish amount of turn Warne extracted and the extra deviation off the edge, it was a thrill to pouch it.

Wicket-keepers are marked by higher standards than any other cricketing practitioner. If a bowler delivers two full tosses in a row no-one says he can't bowl. If a Test opener makes a pair the worst accusation likely to come his way is that he is out of form.

But a 'keeper only has to misglove a couple of regulation takes a day to be branded sloppy, not just for that performance but for the summer, perhaps for life.

THE LARA INCIDENT

"Do you want your arse broken, man?"

KEITH ARTHURTON TO ME IN SYDNEY, JANUARY 1993

Just after noon on 6 January 1993, I stood in the middle of the Sydney Cricket Ground wicket square and told my Australian team-mates I was ready to retire from Test cricket.

I was at the low point of a summer in which my relationship with the West Indies team had plunged to an icy level; it has never recovered and I have not been in a West Indian dressing room since that day.

I could only stand and watch as umpires Darrell Hair and Terry Prue consulted over the merits of what should have been the most routine of dismissals—West Indian Carl Hooper bowled by Shane Warne. I said to the boys in a quiet but firm tone, "If this is given not out I am retiring." It was no gee-up or idle threat.

Warnie's sharp-turning leg-break had beaten the outside edge of Hooper's bat, after he played back, and brushed the top of the off-stump. Normally in such circumstances a stump will rock back but because the stumps were set so firmly in a flint hard pitch and the ball only tickled it, there was no big movement.

I took the ball after the impact, then instinctively motioned my gloves back towards the stumps—it's second nature for 'keepers to do that, a reflex motion that we've all seen a thousand times—before galloping off towards Warne for the celebration.

I only let out a half-hearted appeal, behaving in the way you do when a batsman has been bowled, or the decision is clear-cut.

But Hooper stood his ground, and this prompted the umpires to debate whether the bails had been dislodged by the ball or my gloves. The fact that I considered the decision a formality—and in these situations the 'keeper invariably knows what has happened—seemed to mean nothing to them.

And that's what hurt.

The replay on the giant SCG scoreboard showed there was no doubt about the dismissal, but the umpires chatted on. Fair enough, they shouldn't be influenced by the scoreboard replay, but my emotions became a potent cocktail of frustration, embarrassment and anger.

Finally, to my immense relief, Hooper was sent on his way.

However, it was not this incident, in isolation, which was the core of my discontent.

The key factor was that it was the third time that summer my credibility had been questioned and, feeling mistrusted and tarnished, I had simply had enough.

Cricket, the game which I had pursued with such passion since my days in short pants at Biloela, had suddenly become a dark, grimly serious and not very enjoyable grind. It was to take me months of soul searching to feel at peace with myself and my future. The first and most traumatic incident had been the Brian Lara dismissal in the First Test in Brisbane when I muffed a stumping chance from Lara off Greg Matthews. The second blow to my self-esteem was when I snared what I considered a low, but relatively straight-forward catch behind from Keith Arthurton in the same Test.

The Lara affair occurred late on the second day of the Test when Austra-lia and the West Indies were locked in a full strength arm wrestle. Australia had made 293 and Lara and Keith Arthurton had combined confidently for a fourth wicket union of 112 to take the tourists to the safe, if not high ground of 3–170.

Bowling around the wicket, Greg Matthews delivered a beautifully flighted ball which initially looked easy meat for leg-side runs, but then drifted so late and wide I had to reach almost a metre outside the leg stump to try to haul it in.

With Lara, normally the most graceful of batsmen, advancing, over-bal-ancing, then stumbling to the deck, I reached too far for the ball, which hit me on the wrists then dropped to the turf.

With Lara still out of his ground, I tried to recover the ball three times but as I tumbled over my gloves pushed the ball past the stumps and towards the off-side. Matthews, watching in hope, rocked his head back and grabbed his then limited supply of hair.

I now concede after watching videos of the incident that the ball made no contact with the stumps, that my right glove disturbed the stumps as I swooped at the ball. But at the time I was unsure whether the ball had hit the stumps.

Yet square leg umpire Terry Prue, who must have been unsighted because my tumbling body was blocking his line of sight, raised his finger to signify Lara was out. Perhaps he was watching the crease—of which he had a clear view—for the one concrete factor about the issue was that Lara was short of his ground.

The start of the worst moment in my cricket career.
The controversy over the Brian Lara stumping decision at the Gabba
in 1992-93 boiled over into acrimony in the dressing rooms.

The whole episode became instantly dramatic, with Prue walking in from square leg to chat with us while Lara, quite theatrically, stayed lying on the pitch with his bat outstretched into the crease as he looked up in hope for a reversed decision. He was eventually helped to his feet by Arthurton.

Lara looked at me as if to say, "What's the story?" I knew my glove had brushed the stumps, but as I tumbled I had lost sight of the ball and probably closed my eyes.

I had not appealed, rather I held out my arms in a gesture of bewilderment as if to say, "I don't know what happened." Mark Taylor, who was at first slip said the ball had not hit the stumps, information which was relayed to umpire Prue, who said, "I saw the ball hit the stumps." And that is where I left the matter.

If only we could go back in time. On reflection I would overrule the umpire 10 times out of 10—even if there was only a modicum of doubt.

Unfortunately I didn't do so and have had to live with the consequences.

Team manager Ian McDonald was adamant that I face the media, because he remembered the fracas which followed the decision to ban my Australian predecessor Greg Dyer from talking about his dropped catch off New Zealand's Andrew Jones a few years earlier. The ball had fallen from Greg's grasp as he attempted a diving interception, but he'd regathered it mid-tumble and Jones was adjudged out. Dyer's career never recovered.

As I contemplated my own fate I reflected on Dyer's and thought how unfortunate it was that he never had the opportunity to give his side of the story. How could they just leave him to roast?

Incidents should be handled by allowing the accused to speak his mind. At the press conference questions flew quickly.

- Did I know the ball had not hit the wicket? "I had no idea of where the ball had gone—initially I was very disappointed to drop it."
- What did I say to Terry Prue? Did anyone tell me the ball had missed the stumps? "Myself and Mark Taylor told the umpire my gloves had hit the stump."
- What did I say to Lara? "Brian said to me, 'C'mon' and I said, 'Look where I am, I haven't got a clue.' I don't know how it looks on video but I can't recall what the ball had done. I remember picking up my hat, looking at Brian and hearing the crowd go berserk. Obviously by then he had been given the decision."
- Was there any consideration given to calling Lara back? "I've got no idea. The umpire was told what happened and he has given the decision. I don't know whether it is up to us to recall him."
- Will the incident upset the team? "I wouldn't think the team would be but this is unsettling to me."

Determined to ensure there were no lingering bad vibes, I shared a dressing room chat with Lara after stumps. We even watched the incident on the news. When we left each other's company that night there seemed no bitter vibes.

But my relationship with the West Indies side, particularly Lara, was never the same again. I spoke to Lara briefly during the 1995 tour there, but he no longer seems comfortable in my company. He does not warm to me.

It's unfortunate but I can live with it.

My anguish intensified on the third morning of play when Prue released a statement effectively distancing himself from my remarks, which were emblazoned in Brisbane's *Sunday Mail* under a massive headline saying "I'M INNOCENT" and, in smaller type, "We told umpires it was with my glove."

Prue's statement simply said, "I accept that Australian players stated the stumps were broken by Ian Healy's gloves, however, I would like to stress at no stage did I hear any player inform me of this. I believe it is important this fact is made clear and I now consider the matter closed."

So I said one thing, and Prue said another. It gnawed away at me that the matter ended there, totally open-ended. In my view I was left to carry a soiled reputation and I wasn't happy. You would have thought some sound-thinking official would suggest "Let's get them together in front of the press and sort it out."

My character was being questioned; my diaries felt
the full weight of my self-doubt.

It would not have worried me.

The Arthurton "catch" incident came the day following the Lara incident. This was just a dreadful decision by Prue. It was a routine outside edge from Steve Waugh's bowling accepted comfortably above the ground. We just took for granted it was going to be given out. Arthurton was 72 at the time and progressed to an ultimately decisive 178 not out.

The decision was worse than the Lara verdict the day before and I took it very personally.

My rapport with the West Indies reached the depths two Tests later in Sydney when I followed the rest of the boys into the West Indian dressing room to congratulate Lara after his great innings of 277. It was essentially a "test the water" exercise after the Brisbane fiasco and I found the temperature sub-zero.

A few of the Windies players started laughing in a "Well, well, look who's here" manner when I walked in. Then Arthurton, who simply doesn't get along with our side, piped up with "Do you want your arse broken, man?"

The rest of the Windies seemed to support him. My initial reaction was one of anger at how a player of Arthurton's limited experience could carry on in such an audacious, demeaning manner.

The West Indies' dislike of me was laid bare and though their feelings were laced with bitterness and acrimony, at least they were out in the open. I walked out of that West Indies dressing room and have not returned since.

In a perverse way I emerged from that flashpoint with a special peace of mind. If I had not made that trip I would have forever wondered what they were thinking about me.

I am the sort of person who likes to feel liked and wanted. That's just my personality. As I have become older, harder and more experienced I don't care as much what people think of me and I have no problems with being genuinely detested by the opposition. There are plenty of times in sport when someone in your side has to take a few bullets. This time it was me.

But at that stage I really wanted to be liked and was copping it from everywhere. My depressed state of mind was evident in this diary entry made immediately after the Sydney Test.

> My integrity was questioned yet again when Hooper was bowled. I have got very serious about what's happening ... near retirement. I must sort the situation out. I can't continue to let it worry me.
>
> I must accept people are split in their opinions on me and get on with life. A 'keeper's lot is in amongst it and I can't back away from it. I must lighten up about it and accept it as part of my job and contribute to a team victory no matter what. I now dislike the opposition.

I started to develop a mild paranoia. The question of my tarnished credibility was entering my mind in every relationship I had. Even when I was stopped by a member of the public in the street my initial emotion was one of suspicion at what that person really thought of me. I even started to wonder what my family and friends were thinking of me as well.

I did not clear my head until mid-January, when I decided to sit down and write out the pros and cons of continuing to play Test cricket.

The pros were a mile long, simple things like guaranteeing a good living for my family, enjoying the mateship, being part of a successful side.

And the cons were things I would live with, such as being disliked by the opposition. But I just needed to see it on paper to convince myself I wanted to go on.

One of the worst things in the game for me is taking things too personally. These sorts of problems hit me hard. My demeanour within the team during those months was conspicuously depressed. There is always some sort of gee-up running through the team but none of the boys were game to stir me about the Lara dismissal, because they were well aware of my acute sensitivity on the topic.

The showdown in the Sydney dressing room was a sobering face slap for me; it made me determined to get going again, to get focused after a couple of months when my thoughts had drifted to peripheral matters.

I thought, "Bugger it." I was not going to waste nervous energy fretting about what they thought of me. It was time to get on with life.

But I made a pair in the Fourth Test in Adelaide, that famous gut-wrencher when Craig McDermott and Tim May shared a reviving but ultimately fruitless last wicket stand that ended when Craig gloved one behind off Courtney Walsh when we needed two for victory.

To fail to score a run in either innings when we were beaten by a solitary run did little for my sagging spirits.

I wrote in my diary:

I am so depressed about my batting and general persona ... negative, internal and quiet.

I have never had a history of being scared of being dropped. This has reduced my intensity and performance. So what? I failed with the bat. Get on with it and keep throwing punches. Enjoy training and play in order to be a positive influence on all.

Don't take the easy option of giving it all up. Maintain a positive focus and work hard and be bubbly all match.

But it was hard to stay bubbly all match in the final Test in Perth—we were simply slaughtered by an innings and 25 runs on a wicket containing such vicious bounce that the groundsman who produced it later lost his job.

Curtly Ambrose had bowled well all series, but he suffered from an ailment that had occasionally afflicted Carl Rackemann, in that he was often bowling a metre too short and found his better deliveries were beating the bat rather than catching the edge.

In Perth he pitched the ball further up to the bat and snared a breathtaking 7–1 with six of his victims, yours truly included, caught behind or in slips. Ambrose generated some bizarre statistics in that series, including the fact that Steve Waugh did not hit him for one Test match four all summer.

He never spoke to the Australians, preferring that we know as little as possible about him. The West Indies described him as the sort of player who didn't particularly like cricket, who would mentally clock off at 6pm and didn't clock on until 11am the next day. But he was such a great professional that he never even bowled a bad spell in the nets.

At the end of that season we visited New Zealand before the England tour and at Christchurch a spectator put up a sign saying "Be honest, Mr Healy", which McDermott ripped down before play.

It had been the toughest season of my career, yet the scales were about to balanced, for great rewards were to be reaped at our next stop: England, 1993.

THE GLORY

"An Ashes tour to us is the most important thing in our lives—
it's up to England to match that passion."

ALLAN BORDER

Sombre is not a bleak enough word to describe the mood in the bar of Sydney's Sheraton hotel the night of 29 March 1993 ... if you were a Queenslander.

The Maroons, chasing what would have been our first ever Sheffield Shield, were skittled for 75 in a final against New South Wales at the Sydney Cricket Ground.

That night was a time for Queenslanders to console each other after yet another end of season tailspin, yet when the Australian side jumped on a flight from Auckland earlier that day, at the end of our short tour of New Zealand Queensland had just started their second innings.

As we were about to land a couple of hours later the plane's captain announced New South Wales would wrap up the Shield first thing in the morning. I was dumbstruck. I can remember Steve Waugh letting out a joyous yelp as I surged forward in the plane to ask the captain to confirm this soul-destroying news.

So our drink that night became more of a wake for another fruitless season rather than the late match pep-up I had hoped it would be.

I settled into the company of former Queensland and Australian wicket-keeper John Maclean and former Queensland fast bowler Sandy Morgan, who like his brother Paul, chairman of the Brisbane Broncos and corporate trouble-shooter, loves a chat and tossing out a few opinions. Naturally, the conversation turned to the upcoming Ashes tour of England.

He said to me, "The problem with your batting is that you have got the typical 'keeper's batting syndrome. You are happy with 30 and 40 and then get out. You don't think of yourself as a batsman. You also get caught behind the wicket a lot, in the slips or gully."

Right, I do tend to go a little hard at things outside off stump, but I made the point that I reckoned I was up to a Test century. So we agreed that whenever I got out for less than 30, caught in the slips, he would ring me up in England to reinforce his theory, but I was allowed a reverse charge phone call to him when I scored my first Test century in England.

It was a bold prediction on my part. I had never scored a century in first class cricket, never mind in Tests, and I had not been in great touch recently at Test level, having made three ducks in my last four Test innings against the West Indies in Australia that summer.

In fact there were quiet whispers I needed runs to keep Tim Zoehrer's challenge for my spot at bay when I lined up against England in the First Test at Old Trafford.

That Test is still remembered for "that ball"—Shane Warne's unforgettable first ball to Mike Gatting, the perfect leg-spinner which, after starting on a leg-stump line, drifted wickedly late in its flight path to land 15 centimetres outside leg stump and snap back to hit off.

Gatt, totally bewildered, momentarily stood his ground. The look he gave me seemed to say, "Did you tickle the stumps with your gloves?"

So, a century, and Sandy Morgan's conversation, were the last things on my mind when I walked to the crease in the second innings with Australia 5–230, effectively 5–309. It was a position of comfort, if not control, one where every run we scored hurt England's chances deeply.

My role was clear ... support Steve Waugh, who had come to the crease half an hour earlier. There simply would not be time for me to make a big total because this was early on the fourth day.

We would attempt to make a nice little partnership to put the game beyond England's reach.

Maybe Steve saw something in my demeanour that day which bode well for my prospects. I had barely reached 20 when he said to me, "This is going to be your day, today. It's century time." I said, "Get out of it ..." but there were little signposts saying this was indeed going to be my day.

After reaching 50, I got a short ball from Phil DeFreitas. England had two men back less than 30 metres apart waiting for my occasionally infamous hook shot. The toughening up process in cricket at international level can be painful and ongoing, and it took me a long time to work out how and when to play the hook shot responsibly.

Mum had been advising me from childhood not to hook until I was at 50, and one night after I was out hooking in Adelaide she was on the phone saying, "What have I told you about the hook shot?"

I am sorry to admit I hung up on her—but how was she to know that I had spent the entire week practising how to better cope with the short ball?

At Old Trafford my placement was centimetre perfect and the fieldsmen crossed over in despairing dives as the ball thundered into the fence.

I reached the 90s and asked Steve how I should approach my century. He plumbed the depths of his cricketing wisdom and offered the following: "Stuffed if I know. I've bombed out about five times in the 90s. Why don't you try and get there with a six."

Two fours in consecutive balls off Phil DeFreitas sufficed. The second one was off the prototype English seamer's delivery pitched just outside off stump on a nice length. On other days I might have offered a limp defensive bat but Steve was right—that day was my day. I thumped it over mid-on.

It remains a beautiful memory.

One of my first phone calls home was to Sandy Morgan, and my smile was mischievous as I requested the reverse charge call ...

But Sandy's wife refused me my moment in time—she told the operator Sandy was out walking the dog, and hung up.

The faxes rolled in, 104 of them. I remember lying in bed in the darkness and hearing them being passed under the door. I couldn't wait until morning to read them, so I gathered them up and took them into the toilet to read so as not to disturb my room-mate, Tim Zoehrer.

I had waited 101 first class matches for my first century and the joy it gave me was enhanced by the heartfelt congratulations. They came from far and wide—Dean Jones, then playing at Durham, Sri Lankan batsman Asanka Gurusinha, and old friends at Biloela.

I had once given a bottle of Moet Chandon to Andrew Slack, the former Wallaby, for helping me with a video, and he had promised he'd only crack it open when I scored my first Test century. He faxed me to say he had!

There was one from John Maclean, saying, "Sandy Morgan has already contacted me, claiming credit for inspiring you to this performance."

Then finally, one from Sandy which said, "You are a genius. Sorry I wasn't at home this morning. You are now a batsman-wicketkeeper, not a wicket-keeper-batsman ... like that?"

And Simmo told me he could not have been prouder if I was his son, saying I'd kept my head. "Ian often just bats faster and faster until he gets out," he once said about my batting. That remains the best Test of my career. I can barely recall misgloving a ball, yet it would have been easy to do so on the last day as part of a letdown after my century.

I recorded the last day of the Test in my diary quite simply as "a great day in my life", and indeed it was.

Such moments are golden ones in the life of a cricketer. Those faxes were like a pep pill for the rest of the tour for a player who only five months before was contemplating quitting the game.

Boonie gave me big wraps all night as we celebrated our win and, despite being a pacesetter in the drinking stakes, performed an astonishing feat of athletic balance when challenged by Merv and a high-powered fire hydrant.

Stunned by the force of the blast, Boonie was blown backwards and into a pot plant, yet quite incredibly, he managed to not spill a drop of the beer he was carrying in his right hand or dampen the cigarette carried in his left

Steve Waugh said to me, "This is your day," and he was right—as usual.

hand. When the hydrant was turned off, he simply got to his feet and carried on drinking and smoking, despite the fact that he looked like the Abominable Snowman.

I remember sledging Boonie about the fact that he still hadn't scored a Test ton in England. "Keep going mate, you'll get there one day," I said.

The 1993 tour left an indelible mark on the careers of our two great fast bowlers, Merv Hughes and Craig McDermott. There is no doubt in my mind that it left Merv psychologically burnt out. Displaying admirable courage, he battled a knee injury throughout the summer, but the price for his perseverance was missing most of the next season.

After the incredible stress of playing with the injury for three months, he just couldn't regenerate psychologically, couldn't get back up the mountain.

He did play for Australia again—in South Africa at the end of the next season—but he wasn't at his peak, physically or psychologically.

I regard him as a genuine champion of our era; my lingering memory of Merv is a defining moment of the 1993 series.

In the Old Trafford Test the final ball of the second last day was bowled by Merv. We had struggled to break through the Poms, who had advanced to 1–133.

That ball was angled into Gatting from a widish angle outside off-stump and he played awkwardly across the line, missed and was bowled.

He kicked the ground in disgust as photographers snapped what was one of the enduring shots of the summer—Merv Hughes giving AB a vice-like bear hug mid-pitch. There were no other figures in the background—just Gatt's disturbed stumps with middle stump on a drunken tilt.

The wicket typified Merv's ability to take a big scalp when it was needed in the series and underlines why I rate him the best competitor I have played with.

McDermott's fate came as a real shock. In the Lord's Test we had declared at 4–632 then had to set about the long road to victory without Craig, who had been taken ill and was in a small room out the back of the dressing room. Just how ill he was we didn't realise and, when we heard a groan of pain someone yelled out, "Tell him the wicket's not that flat." Our mood soon changed when the full extent of the problem became known and he was dramatically rushed to hospital for a bowel operation.

Early in the tour, during the first one-dayer, the Manchester crowd had started up an "Ee-aw" chant when McDermott was at the bowling crease. It stemmed from an earlier misfield, when they started calling him a donkey.

None of us took much notice of it but because Craig did, and made a point out of it, our mischievous side was tickled. Craig interpreted it as a slur on him and, upon re-entering the dressing room announced, "I've worked it out … it's my (donkey) ears."

We were surprised that (a) he would take any notice of the chant and (b) that he would admit to having abnormally large "wingnuts".

Soon afterwards Steve 'Tugga' Waugh and Maysie were passing a toy shop and couldn't resist buying 11 pairs of extra-large plastic ears they saw on display. We snuck them onto the field up our jumpers in our county game against

Gloucestershire and, while Craig was walking back to his mark to bowl, put them on.

As he was running into bowl the next ball even he saw the funny side of it and broke up laughing.

As if fate was trying to balance the scales for giving me a first Test to remember, I broke my right thumb in that match against Gloucestershire.

It hurt like anything and meant a visit to a specialist for X-rays. The radiographer recommended I take 28 days off so that it had time to heal.

No chance.

Although it was only three days before the next Test and though I was named in the Test 12 on match eve I had written in my diary, "This is the first time I have doubted (my chances of playing) ... ever."

But there are times in a sportsman's life when you simply have to turn your back on medical advice and front up for a major match.

We won the Lord's Test by an innings minus Craig McDermott and with only three specialist bowlers. It was an exceptional feat and Tim May was quivering with excitement when he joined our huddle after catching Graham Gooch in the outfield. He was so pumped he gave us the benefit of some of his famous dry wit, making out things were moving so rapidly it was impossible to keep track. "Who did we get out ... oh, that Gooch bloke," he said with mock seriousness.

England's bowlers copped a pasting all summer, and the signs were there early that they may have been lacking in confidence—new cap Andy Caddick said, "If things don't work out I'll just go back to Somerset," which seemed a slightly laid-back mentality for a Test new blood.

After two Test defeats—seven in a row for England—the newspaper headlines were screaming for changes and targetting selection chairman, Ted Dexter. "Drop the Ted Donkey" said one, a play on words from the television show "Drop the Dead Donkey".

Our county game against Hampshire gave me an insight into the negative thinking that pervades county cricket. We set Hampshire 291 in 64 overs for victory on the last day and they were positively steaming at 0–167, needing an achievable 125 off 23 overs.

They finished 6–220 after calling off the chase, which I felt was inexcusable caution from their captain Mark Nicholas. Mark is a bright man, an experienced and worldly captain and an entertaining journalist who has astute views on the game. That was simply poor cricket. Who cares if Hampshire loses to Australia or Australia loses to Hamsphire?

Both sides owed it to cricket to chase an outright result and Hampshire's failure to do so was most disappointing.

The Third Test at Trent Bridge was my 50th, and the one in which Steve Waugh played the innings he says was the turning point in his career. We were six down at tea on the last day batting only to save the match, but Steve (47 not out), with Brendon Julian (57 not out) at his side, batted throughout the last session to earn us a tense draw after a gripping five day struggle.

Displaying an immaculate defence, he shed all extravagance from his game in a risk-free two hour stay. He was to frustrate bowlers from all nations with a slightly more upbeat version of this technique for the next three years.

In time, it would influence my game as well. The following summer when we were trying to bat out time in a Test against South Africa at Johannesberg, I was in a generally defensive mode but playing the occasional stroke.

Batting partner Steve said to me, "Why are you playing any shots at all?"

I replied, "If I go into my shell I will get out," to which he responded, "You won't, you know."

He was quite right. I found if you bat to avoid getting out you start getting right behind the ball and your game becomes error free.

I enjoyed trying this "no shots" philosophy in the Fourth Test against England at the Adelaide Oval in the 1994–95 summer when I made 51 not out—but not enough to save us from defeat.

The intense pressure of Trent Bridge dissipated two days later when the boys were involved in a betting sting that went the way of most betting plunges. We were playing Minor Counties at Stone and Mark Waugh found a bookmaker offering the sumptuous odds of 16–1 on Australia scoring 200 before lunch.

'Junior's' betting philosophy is that he will put as much on a long shot as a favourite and a quick whip around the dressing room gave us enough money to give the bookie sweaty palms—100 pounds. He almost fell off his stand when we tried to get on and would only take less than half this amount.

Amid a hurricane of rash strokes, we collapsed to 5–97 and our bet never looked like coming off.

During our tour match against Durham Ian Botham retired.

'Both' wanted to play his last game of cricket against his oldest and fondest foes, but it rained overnight after the second day and Both sensed at lunchtime his cricket career had come to a soggy ending. So he passed around the red and white wine and we all had a swig in his honour.

But the clouds cleared and he had to go out and bowl later in the day, striving for a last wicket to remember against the Aussies. But Steve Waugh and Matt Hayden denied him a victim in his last spell, which was described by one paper as probably the worst spell of bowling ever to get a standing ovation.

During his final overs Both said to Matty (hinting a presentation wicket would be in order), "You are the most serious first class cricketer I have ever played against." Matt simply replied, "I just think it's an honour to play against you, for I have always admired you."

The Lara Incident. While I'm scrambling for the ball Brian Lara is scrambling to make good his ground. The doubt that clouded the incident is written over all our faces, mine, Greg Matthews and Lara's. The umpire, Terry Prue, had no doubt.

Previous page: A moment no cricketer ever forgets—that first century in a Test match. And the feeling only gets better if it's against England in the battle for The Ashes. It was at Old Trafford, 1993.

VIV JENKINS/AUSTRALIAN CRICKET BOARD

VIV JENKINS/AUSTRALIAN CRICKET BOARD

Excuse me, 'Clem'! When Wasim Akram edged one from Merv Hughes, Terry Alderman at first slip had it all lined up. But would it carry? My gut feeling said "maybe not", so I went for it, with a happy ending. It was at the MCG, First Test, 1990. Photographer Viv Jenkins won an award for his lightning reflexes.

Overpage: *We've just thrashed England in the Fourth Test at Leeds, 1993, giving us an unbeatable 3-0 series lead, and a hold on The Ashes for another four years. English cricket might be in a mess, but you never let a chance go by to celebrate an Ashes victory.*

ALL SPORT/AUSTRALIAN PICTURE LIBRARY

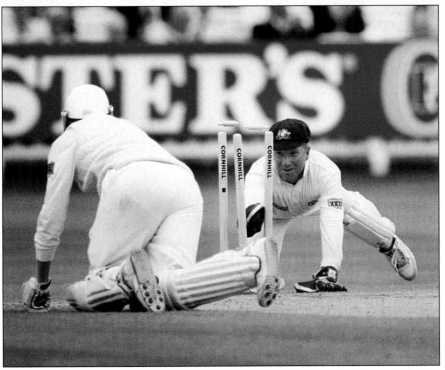

I meet Her Majesty—and three of her cricketers meet their match. It was on the 1993 Ashes tour, and (from top left, anti-clockwise) Graham Gooch got a tickle on a Shane Warne leggie, Matthew Maynard failed to read Tim May's arm-ball and Mike Atherton stumbled and was run out for 99.

You are looking at one of the game's great characters, the irrepressible Mervyn Hughes.
And one of the world's great fast bowlers. The enormous workload he endured on the 1993
Ashes tour (as well as his enormous appetite!) ultimately led to his downfall.

In the Fourth Test at Leeds our batsmen were motivated to make a target out of expatriate Australian Martin McCague, who was born in Ulster but grew up in Port Hedland in Australia's dusty north-west.

He had declared his allegiance to England that summer and gave our players some sharp verbal taunts in the previous Test. He eventually broke down after taking 0–115, figures the boys were happy about.

We eventually made a phenomenal 4–653, with Allan Border cracking 200 not out and Steve Waugh remaining undefeated on 157.

AB did not have to look far for motivation. Match organisers repeatedly and painfully played a video called *Botham's Ashes* over the in-house system featuring, of course, Australia's collapse at Headingley.

After a while it got up everyone's dander, particularly AB's. He kept on saying, "This is unbelievable, that was 12 years ago."

This time at Headingley England lost the Ashes, their captain Graham Gooch resigned to be replaced by Mike Atherton and Australia found a new hero, Paul Reiffel, who took eight wickets for the match.

The Fifth Test at Edgbaston brought an Australian victory by eight wickets, a century to Mark Waugh, a satisfying 80 for me and a slow fuse news story which exploded almost two years later.

Before the start of play on the fifth day, a former Pakistan cricketer offered AB US$500 000 to throw the game.

We were 0–9 chasing 120 for victory. When approached later about it, the offer was laughed off as a joke and he said he had casually dropped it into the conversation after a chance meeting with AB.

That was not the case. AB was summoned from the dressing room and there was no hint of a joke about the incident from AB when he returned. Quite stunned by it, he said, "I've been offered $500 000 to throw the match."

I remember chipping in with, "That's nowhere near enough." I was quite flippant about it because at that stage the cricket world had not taken bribing allegations seriously and was yet to be rocked by the Salim Malik betting scandal which erupted in 1995.

A touching moment came at the end of England's last innings in the Sixth Test at The Oval. The bowlers had performed splendidly on that tour, in Merv Hughes' case often in extreme pain, and after bowling England out for the last time on tour, they left the field together—Merv, Tim May, Shane Warne and Paul Reiffel. The Oval crowd sent them off in style, not with raucous cheering but with sustained, heartfelt applause. They knew exactly why the foursome were walking off together at the head of the pack and their warm salute was appreciated by the players.

THAT MISS

"You can't change your mistake, but you can use it as a challenge."
RUGBY LEAGUE COACH JACK GIBSON

Former boxing great Joe Frazier once said before a world title fight, "If I lose I will walk away and not feel bad because I did all I could to prepare—there was nothing more to do."

I like this theory. From my earliest years, when quizzed by people about my passion for training, I often explained that I was driven, in part, to prepare for the day when I made a mistake that cost Australia a Test match.

If that day ever arrived, I simply didn't want team-mates firing an accusing glance at me that said, "You could have trained harder."

My black day came in Pakistan in 1994 when I missed a last ball stumping off Inzamam-ul-Haq to give Pakistan a one-wicket victory in the first Test of the series in Karachi.

If ever there was a Test to set the pulse on fast forward it was the Karachi one, a tight rope walk featuring occasional slips and sterling revivals and it built up to such a crescendo on the last day the English umpire Dickie Bird, who had stood in the middle for more Tests than any other umpire, rated it the best Test he had seen.

Karachi's National Stadium has long been a devil's playground for visiting sides. In 30 Tests dating back to 1955, Pakistan boasted a proud, unbeaten record of 14 wins and 16 draws. Australia had never won there, nor had they won anywhere in Pakistan for 35 barren years.

And I had my own ledger to balance—Karachi was where I had made a rugged entrance to Test cricket six years before. Pakistan can be a testing place to play cricket for a myriad of reasons. Not the least is the highly excitable nature of the crowds, which leave you with a flutter in your heart all day.

You might be intent on relaxing in the dressing room when suddenly your attention is snatched by a raucous crowd shout. It might only be a bouncer, or a play and miss, but it means that you never quite manage to relax. Matches don't simply roll along like they do in Australia.

A gripping first day typified the character of the game. Australia seemed to be in freefall at 4–99 at lunch yet Michael Bevan, so impressive in his debut tour, played beautifully for 82 in his first Test innings.

I was 54 not out at stumps in a satisfying 7–325, which gave our dressing room a buoyant feel.

Pakistan, after being 1–153, were reeled in to 7–209 at stumps on day two and were eventually bowled out for 256, conceding a deficit of 81.

At the end of the third day we could smell victory—5–181, 262 ahead, the only downer being Mark Taylor completed a pair in his debut Test as captain. Tubsy did not raise his head before reaching the dressing rooms and did not pause to remove his helmet until he'd crossed the boundary rope.

At one stage that day we were 2–172, effectively 2–253 ahead, with Mark Waugh and David Boon making fluent progress. But we were unsettled in the last hour after a collapse of 3–3, in which Mark Waugh was yorked by Waqar Younis for 61 and the brilliant Akram spectacularly claimed Steve Waugh and Michael Bevan for golden ducks in the one over.

I was in such a rush to pad up I forgot to put my inside thigh pad on. So where do you think my first ball, from Waqar Younis hit me? I can still feel it.

Pakistan were set 314 to win and, at stumps on the fourth day, were 3–155. I noted in my diary, "'Keeping well again but drifting a little with the tension."

Then I wrote, "Not the outcome," which was my way of saying to myself, "Just worry about doing your job and don't be distracted by thoughts of winning and losing."

On the fifth day we were smoking. Despite the loss of Glenn McGrath for the final day with a side strain and Tim May early in the day with a kinked neck we stormed through Pakistan's middle order to have them 9–258; we were one wicket from a great victory, Pakistan still needed 56 runs.

Inzamam and Mushtaq Ahmed, with a mixture of aggressive and fortunate strokeplay whittled their ask to just three runs; the home crowd cheered every run and chanted Allah-O-Akbar ("God is great").

We left a gap for Inzamam at deep mid-wicket against Warnie in the hope that he would swish across the line and perhaps get a leading edge or simply miss the ball.

Warne, with Australia's fate left in his spinning fingers, bowled the perfect ball. It pitched on leg stump and Inzamam advanced, attempting to strike it through the mid-wicket gap. But he wasn't to the pitch of the ball and, sensing trouble, he started to adjust his shot to cover the ball at the last moment. The ball kept less than knee high, and went below my gloves and through my legs—which were an instant later to feel just like jelly!

The ball was a metre past me before my gloves moved and, as it skuttled off to the fence, I rocked back my head in horror.

I hurt like I had never hurt before.

In total despair I kicked over the stumps and as I retreated towards the dressing room resisted the temptation to put my right boot into a fielding helmet lying 10 metres behind the stumps.

Tubsy Taylor still had his arms outstretched skyward, the other players stood still with hands clutching heads.

Shane Warne's 8–150 in the match won him the man-of-the-match award, but he had the bowed head of a man who had just lost his life's savings. Back in the dressing room, I sat like a zombie, expressionless on the bench.

I wrote of the incident in my diary, "F— it ... unbelievable feeling (numb, can't talk). The game we shouldn't have lost. Started to speak an hour or so after stumps. Can't believe we lost. Must now get on with it. Use it as an experience ... life's realities experienced from the canvas."

The last line came from a fax sent by the head of Australia Post in Queensland, Cliff Richards, which really hit a chord with me. It said:

The last moment of any major sporting event does not decide the out-come. Earlier events contribute to the end result. We understand how you feel because we have all been there in some form or another.

Success stories all have their times of despair. I like to relate such events in life to boxing by saying that anybody who has not spent time in the square ring of life flat on their back looking up at the big lights has not really experienced the realities of life.

What sorts the champions out is that they all know how to beat the dreaded ten count, get up, box on and take it from there.

Now is the time to look forward and treat the past for what it is—an experience. We are all with you and certainly do not think you should be shouldering all the responsibility.

Upon entering a silent dressing room, I didn't say much for a very sound reason ... I couldn't talk. In a bizarre sort of way, I felt like a patient slowly coming to after being sent to sleep for a major operation.

There were shadowing figures moving in slow motion around me and voices echoing through the humidity. It was as if I was in an emotional bubble which no one could penetrate until it was time for me to come out.

Steve Waugh tells a story of watching me sit on the bench gazing stone-faced toward nothing in particular.

He thought it was such an absorbing pose he extracted his ever-present camera from his team kit and walked in front of me with the intention of gaining one of the ten million photos he takes on each tour.

But he couldn't do it. Gripped by a pang of guilt and fear that I would erupt if he took my photo, he decided to leave me be and put his camera back in his bag.

My pain was accentuated because so much was at stake. It was not just a missed chance somewhere during the last day, and it didn't just allow them to escape to a draw. It was the last ball and the margin was between victory and defeat.

We went to a reception at the British Embassy that night and at one point I blew up and cried for a short period. After that the mood lightened and things never seemed so bad again.

A team-mate from my Brisbane club, Norths, Dominic Ovenden faxed me: "Just remember, if they give you the arse over there, I might be able to find you a spot in our first grade team."

And I thought, "Well, I have completed my player profile now. I have finally a 'biggest disappointment in cricket'."

I couldn't sleep that night. The only scene replayed in my mind, over and over, was that last ball. Each time I made the stumping. I knew at last how Tim May felt about the day in Adelaide when he and Craig McDermott took Australia to within one run of victory against the West Indies in 1993. Every day or so Maysie thinks about that and how he could have scored an extra run.

I still think about that miss every so often, but time has mellowed the pain and I reflect on other things that happened in the game which could have cost our side victory.

But how I would have loved to have made that stumping. It was a chance a career could have been built on—remember that Test and you'd remember the stumping and the 'keeper who made it.

Why did I miss it?

Inzamam gave a clue when he said, "It pitched outside leg, turned and I missed it. I thought I was bowled." I saw it go past his bat and I saw him move his feet. Basically I was not watching the ball as well as I would have liked. I thought it was going to hit the stump. If your eyes don't come back to the ball once it spins past the bat you are in trouble. The height wasn't a problem. I wish I had focused on that ball a little better.

This type of mistake happens to all 'keepers occasionally, no matter how much you practise or how good your form is at the time.

You just hope it doesn't happen on the last ball of a Test match when you need one wicket for victory.

The Karachi Test was also notorious for another incident. It transpired that on the fourth night of play, the night before that fatal last day, Shane Warne picked up his phone at the Pearl-Continental hotel to receive a call which would later send his life into a spin.

Pakistan captain Salim Malik summoned Warnie to his room and offered him and Tim May an unbelievable sum each to bowl poorly on the last day and thus ensure a Pakistan victory. Malik allegedly claimed it would be an embarrassment for Pakistan to lose the Test.

Warnie and Maysie took the action any self-respecting sportsman would take and ignored the offer.

The funny thing is neither I, nor any member of the team, foresaw the

STEVE WAUGH

When in Karachi ... the boys decided a little bit of local colour would
be in order on the 1994 Pakistan tour, in the form of moustaches and beards.
Simmo, far left, won the Jack Palance award.

magnitude of the shock the incident would send rocking around the cricket world over the next year.

When we found out about it, the team's initial reaction was one of mild amusement. Players were joking about the offer without giving any real thought to the scandalous lack of integrity behind it. To us it was so bizarre it was almost comical.

People ask: why weren't you hostile to Malik for the rest of the series? Simply because, in a naive sort of way, we didn't know how big the big picture really was.

We only got dark months later when the credibility of Warne, and co-accusers Tim May and Mark Waugh was challenged after they had offered statements containing details of the bribe offers, and the whole affair dissolved into a vitriolic administrative dogfight. Warne and May became quite deeply affected by the saga.

When Malik subsequently toured Australia in1995–96 he was brushed by the entire Australian team, with not a solitary word passing from our lips in his direction all tour.

What could you say to him? There was no way I wanted to say anything and I am reminded by sagely words of my mother: "If you can't say something nice to someone, don't say anything at all."

Did Malik fear retribution when he came to Australia for the 1995–96 series? During the Brisbane Test he had to go off after splitting the webbing on his hand in the field. The word is that when a local doctor suggested he needed an injection to minimise the risk of infection, Malik said, "You will try and poison me." Paranoia, or a joke?

Once he'd left Australia he seemed to toughen up a bit. In an interview during the World Cup he claimed that Warne had approached him for a chat during the Australian tour, "but I told him to piss off".

No such conversation ever took place.

The whole affair raises doubts about the results against Pakistan over the years. Before our quarter final against New Zealand in the 1996 World Cup I had an interesting chat to a former Indian spinner.

He told me about a Test match played in the late 1970s where India scored 331 in their first innings. According to the spinner the rumour was that the punters had put plenty on a first innings lead by India.

Home alone. If I thought Lady Luck had only temporarily deserted me when I missed the vital stumping of Inzamam in the First Test, I was wrong. Before the Third I was on the plane out of Pakistan, my thumb broken.

Imagine how much quicker the rumour mill was grinding then when Pakistan declared four wickets down for 272, 59 runs short of India's total. It was a decision that defied commonsense—it meant Pakistan would have to bat last in the Test on a deteriorating wicket.

That's the problem with the Malik business: who is now to say that Pakistan's gloves were raised for every encounter and that some were not soiled by the sinister hands of Bombay bookmakers?

A lot of Pakistan players pull out of games far too easily for my liking. The only certainty of the Malik case is that it will leave an immoveable cloud of suspicion hovering over any poor performance by the Pakistan team. Any sudden form reversal will have curious fans turning a suspicious eye towards the secret betting houses of Bombay.

Two days after Pakistan's World Cup loss to India, a neighbour of Pakistan's captain Wasim Akram lodged a complaint with the high court, stating that Akram had taken money to withdraw from the game.

The next Test in Rawalpindi started two days later. We were under a lot of pressure in the Second Test to do everything perfectly. I was thinking about my footwork throughout the Test, which meant I wasn't performing naturally. The more I started thinking about my feet the slower they moved.

We drew the Second Test and a miserable tour reached its depths in Rawalpindi, this time in the triangular one day series when a ball from Craig McDermott scuttled along the ground and bounced up out of footmarks to break my left thumb.

I knew I was in trouble because it was too painful to put the glove back on once it was taken off.

My string of 64 successive Tests, as well as my finger, was broken. I was sent home.

THE WARNE PHENOMENON

"Shane is the best thing to happen in world cricket for 30 years."
FORMER AUSTRALIAN CRICKET COACH BOB SIMPSON

When I first 'kept to Shane Warne in an Australian XI game in Hobart in 1990 he reminded me of an old-fashioned, home-spun, bush leg-spinner ... in a way he still does.

You know, the feisty old tradesmen you find spinning a web on a Saturday afternoon in any bush ground where the sparsely grassed surface is as hard as Ayers Rock and crisply hit boundaries travel a "country mile". The type of bush legend whose last action before taking the field is to stub out his cigarette and hitch his trousers above a well-nourished waistline that's been expanded by a hardy lifetime's supply of cold beers and warm pies. But the sort of bloke who, come pressure time, you know can play. The ball comes out of his hand well and he knows where every delivery will land. And he can do it all on a lightish preparation.

Warnie may be more streamlined than he used to be and he might have never played a game of bush cricket. But there is something about this type of cricketer I still see in him.

Don't ever expect him to publish a book called *Shane Warne's Guide to Healthy Eating for the Modern Leg-spinner,* for his idea of a balanced diet is a cheeseburger in each hand. But if he does, it should be quite a read, for his culinary tastes are all his own. On long flights to England I have seen him knock back five business class meals to have cheese and crackers all the way.

McDonald's staff across Australia have raised their eyes at his curious habit of ordering two cheeseburgers without the beef patty and putting chips and sauce on the roll.

There are times on tour when you wonder where on earth he can get enough vitamins to stay afloat, for he hardly seems to eat any vegetables or fruit. Yet this is part of the enigma of the man.

The one food that turns his blood sour is mushrooms and he has been known to vomit and start sweating when he thinks he has eaten one. Once in England I put a mushroom on a plate beside him when he got up to serve himself at a buffet and he blew up when he returned. Steve Waugh took the prank a step further when he took a bite out of a mushroom and put in on top of Shane's spaghetti bolognaise while he was away. Steve told Warnie he must have taken a bite out of it without realising and Shane just pushed his meal away and started sweating and fretting.

I have seen him go for a couple of days without eating when the food available wasn't what he liked. During our 1994 tour of Pakistan I roomed with him in the outback province of Multan, home town of Inzamam-ul-Haq and best known for burial grounds and dust.

The first thing he said to me was that he hadn't eaten for two days. There was no room service, but the concierge sent some-one out to get us a packet of potato crisps which, to our lament, were stale. So Warnie's fast was extended by a night.

'Keeping to Shane has been one of the most intriguing, challenging and enjoyable experiences of my career.

I've appreciated it in the same way that an artist who has spent most of his time doing black and white sketches is invigorated by the greater challenge of a full palette of colours. It gives you a chance to showcase your full worth as a craftsman.

He is the most challenging bowler I have ever gloved. Recently I overheard a couple of senior umpires talking about the extreme mental demands of umpiring to Warne during one of his marathon spells on a turning Sydney Cricket Ground wicket.

Warnie and I practise team bonding.

One umpire said he walked off the SCG and headed straight for a table, where he collapsed and ordered two Panadols to soothe a headache generated by a day of intense concentration as he attempted to read every ball of spin bowling's greatest magician.

Another umpire said he felt just as weary after the same experience and was in bed asleep after a quick room service meal by 8.45pm. I can understand their lot just as they could understand mine.

I don't find him quite as taxing because I see him more often, and consequently can read him better, but there are times when the days are long.

Once in Bermuda immediately after the '95 Windies tour, a middle order batsman who found Warnie impossible to read spun on his heel and whispered, "This bloke's a lot easier to read on spin vision."

Then there was the cavalier approach of South African No 11 Fanie de Villiers, who would smile and say, "What will it be today, a six or are you going to get a stumping?" Once in Pakistan when I stumped Fanie in a one-day tournament he turned and said, "Ah dear, you've got me again." Fanie wasn't into the subtleties of playing spin. De Villiers versus Warne in one-day cricket was always a death or glory affair.

But, verbally at least, it was never worth a tailender's while to display too much bravado.

In Sydney in 1994 Warnie came around the wicket to the eccentric South African off-spinner Pat Symcox and spun the ball sharply across the body.

Symcox's remedy was to thrust out his front pad and on one occasion, after padding a ball away, he hollered to Warne, "You'll never get through there, boy."

The very next ball Symcox had the indignity of being bowled by Warne ... not around his legs but through them, which is even more embarrassing. People watching the dismissal on television couldn't understand why the boys celebrated as if we had just dismissed Brian Lara for a first ball duck.

Mystery balls aside, this is Shane Warne's repertoire as I see it.

LEG-SPINNER

His stock ball ... when he is bowling well it drifts towards the leg side and becomes not only his best delivery, but one of the game's most feared weapons for the sheer amount of turn he puts on the ball. In essence it is a three-dimensional ball and no coaching manual can fully tutor a batsman to play it. The batsman's first sighting of it tells him the ball will land on middle stump and so his head and feet are moved accordingly. Once it drifts to leg the batsman tends to find himself out of position and off-balance. The final twist arrives when the ball screws back across the body, often luring a rushed jab which provides a catch for close in fieldsmen. When Warne gains drift batsmen tend to be reluctant to leave their crease against him and once they become crease bound he can dictate terms to them and often get away with a bad ball. Where he lands his leg-spinner depends on conditions and the batsman. If the wicket is turning greatly he needs to pitch it outside leg to have the batsman playing at the ball. If it is not spinning he can bring his line back to middle stump. On certain occasions, such as when Graham Gooch was at the crease, he was justified in taking his line even wider outside off stump, for Graham never played this type of delivery well. So well-refined is Warne's radar that he can consistently vary his game plan to batsmen at different ends without his rhythm being thrown out of kilter. An outside edge of Warne's sharp-turning leg-spinner is the most challenging chance for me off his bowling.

TOP-SPINNER

It is a very important delivery for Shane against left-handers who like to hit with Warne's natural turn through and over midwicket. He produces this ball to lefties in a bid to convince them he is not a one-way bowler and to thwart their bids to dispatch him on the leg side. Richie Benaud has a theory that the top-spinner is a most unsung delivery, one that he used to bowl much more than the wrong 'un and which opened up a host of dismissal opportunities, including lbw and bowled verdicts and catches to short leg from players expecting the leg-spinner. Warne can land his top-spinner at will. Even on flat wickets it gains extra bounce. The extra spin on it can trouble batsmen who hang angular dead bats, as Robin Smith found out when he defended a Warne top-spinner in the 1993 Ashes series but failed to kill the top-spin. The ball screwed back onto his stumps.

WRONG 'UN

I rate his wrong 'un of a satisfactory standard ... but Shane doesn't and that is why he doesn't bowl it as well. He doesn't have full confidence in it. Shane has a theory that it should be as undetectable as his other variations. I don't agree, because even if a batsman knows it is coming, the wrong 'un is still a difficult ball to play. It should be a regular feature of his bowling to left-handers and tail-end batsmen.

FLIPPER

His best variation ball. Shane learnt this wonderful delivery from Jack Potter and Jim Higgs. The flipper has been passed down like a sacred scroll in a line of leg-spinners back to Clarrie Grimmett who invented it in the 1930s. People say Shane's best flippers are the quicker ones, clocked at around 110 kilometres per hour compared to his leggie at 75 kilometres per hour. But I don't agree, for the flipper, a skidding backspinner, is at its most effective when it's bowled at the same tempo as his leg-spinner. Shane can vary the pace and landing point of the flipper to suit the pitch and style of batsman he is confronting. On the slow wickets where the ball grips, such as at Pakistan,

TRENT PARKE/NEWS LTD

Shane Warne so mesmerises batsmen they forget what they're out there for.
Pakistan's Basit Ali tried to play Warnie the way a lot of batsmen have—by shoving
his front pad down the pitch, and keeping the bat out of the way. It worked this time
but eventually, like just about all the others, he perished when he failed to cover the
ball with his pad, exposing his leg stump.

he will bowl it quickly and further up to the batsman, whereas on a fast track like at Perth, he can hold it back and perhaps land it shorter in the hope that the batsman will pull or cut. When South Africa's Darryl Cullinan saw a flipper—perhaps because it doesn't raise much above eye level—something in his subconscious registered, "This is a bad ball." He tried to hit it and after it had foiled him a few times he became circumspect against it and was captured on the crease without moving. So Warne could afford to toss his flipper much further up to Cullinan in an attempt to get him lbw. Occasionally a batsman will bottom edge a flipper. To accept this type of catch generates great satisfaction to know that I have read the ball and stayed down with it.

ZOOTER

A basic back-spinner where he cuts his hand behind the ball. It has a similar trajectory to the flipper. If the wicket is sympathetic to spin, the ball will hit the pitch and hold up. It's a very handy ball which changes the tempo of the pace he bowls. It makes the batsman change his rhythm as well—if he doesn't change he will commit to a false stroke.

At the Melbourne Cricket Ground at the end of the 1995–96 summer, after 'keeping to Shane for more than 2000 overs in international cricket, I batted against him for the first time. Queensland were playing against Victoria in a Sheffield Shield match. It was a fascinating and most enjoyable experience, and reinforced that it is infinitely easier to 'keep than to bat against Warne.

After 'keeping to Shane for four years I felt I knew all there was to know about him but it took only one innings for me to realise the pressure he puts on a batsman is quite different from what I had expected.

He barely spun the ball to me in Melbourne but was bowling really tight. I had a few set plans that I was keen to implement against him, but it struck me that had there been any turn in the wicket, I would have been rendered all but shotless. I hit him for a couple of boundaries because he used some high flighted balls to tempt me—but if the ball had been turning I would have been no chance.

When Warne gains substantial turn almost every shot against him has a high-risk element to it. You need luck and patience.

That innings shaped a few of my thoughts about how Australia should be shaping the attack around him. As Warne is so difficult to score off, we can suffocate batsmen out if the bowler at the other end applies the screws as well.

I feel I can pick Warne 100 per cent on any given day, though obviously throughout a season there will be some mistakes when I get lazy and don't watch him as closely as I should.

So you want to know how I read him? To be totally frank, it's not a matter of me reading him, it's a matter of flicking on a switch somewhere in my subconscious.

Asking me how I read Shane is like asking a touch typist how they hit the right keys.

You have done it so often—in my case hundreds of hours watching and 'keeping to Warne under match and net conditions—that your mind has become programmed.

When I 'keep to Warne I never think, "Right, now this looks like a flipper, I must stay down." Sure, I watch the hand and his demeanour very closely, but my movements are instinctive in the same way that a tennis player might climb after a Boris Becker serve without ever having time to contemplate his actions.

The amount of pressure on Warne is incredible ... I have never seen a cricketer with so many commitments, nor have I seen one handle it so well.

If there is one sure thing about fame it is that it never comes on your terms. Only Warne's closest friends would know the fish bowl life he is occasionally forced to lead. There is a part of him that loves it. The boys are always heckling him about how much he loves the cameras.

In the West Indies he kinked his neck falling off an inflatable banana that was dragged along by a speed boat. News Limited photographer Ray Titus was trailing the boat taking shots. When Shane came to the surface, bad neck and all, his first gesture was to turn towards the camera and say, "Did you get it, Ray?"

For all his talk of mystery balls and spinning secrets, Warne is very gracious in sharing information about his craft, whether he be talking to rival Test leggies Mushtaq Ahmed and Paul Strang or some young leg-spinner at the Australian Institute of Sport.

When he was the guest attraction at the AIS spinner's camp in 1995 he seemed to get a buzz out of working with other leggies and was excited by their potential. Like myself working with 'keepers, Shane finds that the people who know his craft best are those who do it for a living.

He even sat down with David Hookes in the West Indies and, with the assistance of spin cam, explained to the world how he bowled every delivery. Sometimes Shane is far too generous with this information, for there are a few of us who subscribe to the adage that a magician should never reveal how he performs his tricks.

For all of his natural love and awareness of the media spotlight, however, there are times when it can become too much for him and he craves privacy. Shane's parents once declined to give a media interview to a Melbourne newspaper and in a gesture of retaliation the paper published his parents' street address.

For the next few months they were bombarded with calls from the suddenly aware public, an experience which Mr and Mrs Warne found very chastening and uncomfortable. Shane felt their discomfort deeply.

When he visited South Africa it was like Elvis had risen from the dead. Young girls would scream his name whenever he left a venue. If he departed a motel for any length of time there would be up to 20 phone messages from fans and general hecklers when he returned. A group of revellers would knock on his door at 2am after walking into the team motel and somehow locating his room.

When you were rooming with Warnie in the years before we had single rooms you thought, "Oh no." At the distribution of keys at a motel players would ask, "Who's Warnie's secretary?"—that's what it was like to share a room with him.

I am sure the stress from the incredible attention that washed over Warne in South Africa was partly what drove him to snap at the mild-mannered South African opener Andrew Hudson, earning him a $4000 fine from the Australian Cricket Board.

So is Warne a natural or manufactured champion?

I once heard a statement that 95 per cent of champions are normal every-day blokes who became highly motivated. This struck a chord with me. I believe Warne is in the remaining 5 per cent.

Some champions are born champions because of an abnormal physical ability, such as the galloper Phar Lap with his large heart or marathon man Robert de Castella with his freakish lung capacity. Warne has some physical attributes that help his cause, such as large, strong hands, but nothing which should make him ply his trade better than anyone else has done before him.

He didn't take up leg spin until he was 15 and by 22 he was a champion. In these years I don't think he could have been motivated enough to reach such dizzy standards, so it seems to me he must have something special.

However Justin Langer believes that Warne's efforts to improve himself at the Adelaide Cricket Academy were most under-rated. He rated Warne one of the hardest workers there, a player always trying to improve himself.

From my perspective, one of Warne's greatest traits is his ability to inject time and encouragement into others. Many of the game's great players have been self-possessed characters—we all know who they are—so absorbed in their own game they had precious little time for others. And it must be said that it would be much easier to become a star if you spent every waking moment contemplating your own game and don't give a tinker's cuss for your team-mates.

But, to his eternal credit, this could never be said of Warne. I noticed him encouraging others as a youngblood when he first broke into the national team, and I wondered whether he really meant it or whether it was just a mask for an insecure player. But he proved the genuine article and to this day remains a most positive and supportive team member. Whether he is going well or poorly, he still has a lot of time and encouragement for others.

Until Warne emerged it was left to the mid-range players in the team like Geoff Marsh, Peter Taylor and of course, dear old Merv, to establish an ethos of encouragement. When you can get a champion who is a boots and all team man it adds so much to the side.

Friendships mean a lot to Warnie and that's why he cut short a trip to the United States in April, 1996, to attend the funeral of his boyhood hero and friend, St Kilda Australian Rules star Trevor Barker. And in the West Indies in 1995 Warnie's final word to his old mate, Damien Fleming, who broke down and was about to fly home, were, "Love ya, mate." He also rang Flem more often than anyone else, and was always in contact with Merv when he faded out of the international scene.

His friendships with people are solid and he injects quality time into pre-serving them. When Allan Border retired in 1994, the first tour he missed was Pakistan. Again, Warne made more calls to Border than any other player

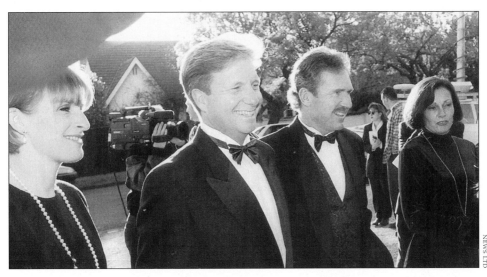

NEWS LTD

The day I saw Shane Warne gripped by nerves—his wedding day to Simone.
Helen and I, and Allan and Jane Border were among the guests.

during that tour. Gestures like this are never taken for granted by ex-cricketers, because they know what life on the cricket train is like.

Players who are dropped or injured often fade from contact, not because anyone wants it that way, but because the current Test players give their full attention to the pressures of the day.

There are two sides to Warnie.

He has a splash of the television detective Colombo in him, in that he comes across as naive but has the knack of subtly asking a probing question that draws a lot of information. I am still to work out whether the naivety is rehearsed or natural. He builds people up nicely and doesn't cut them off if they are telling a story, even if he has heard it before.

The other side of him is that he is quite street smart. He is very rarely left behind in anything. He talks to the Australian Cricket Board about his needs and responsibilities to private sponsors in a way we thought impossible for a player only four or five years into the top class game.

So in some ways he is a man of contrasts, a so-called surfer who's never sat on a board, a grand showman who at other times can display an attractive fondness for the simple pleasures of life. An example of this was Shane's wedding to Simone in 1995 which, for all of Shane's star qualities, was a pleasant low-key affair. He turned down a massive offer from an English company to have it filmed and was not interested in selling his wedding photos to the many Australian women's magazines who were after the photo scoop. But the price of being big business was a dreadful act of betrayal by a photo shop who developed some photos taken by guests at the wedding and sold them to a magazine for a five figure sum.

All he wanted was privacy. Shane's wedding speech had a ring of humility and deep sincerity about it. Among those he thanked most warmly were some buddies from his league cricket days in England who had dug deep into their pockets to make the trip over.

He also made a point of saying how nice his bride looked, "Because at my father's wedding he forgot to say it and Mum has never forgiven him." He was much more nervous that day than I have ever seen him on a cricket field, including the umpteen occasions when he has held our fortunes in his spinning fingers on the last day of a Test. His hands were shaking to the extent that some of the boys started laughing and were offering him a beer.

So let's take a closer look and identify the batsmen who have coped with Warne well.

The top four would be:

ARJUNA RANATUNGA (Sri Lanka)
Sri Lanka's world-wise batsman Asanka Gurusinhe told me recently he believed Ranatunga is the best player of spin in the world. He said over the last 14 years Ranatunga has methodically dissected every spinner he has faced, a fact which previously hadn't dawned on me, but one which I am starting to appreciate. I went back through the history books and saw how Ranatunga had attacked Australia's Bruce Yardley in Colombo in a 1983 Test, how he blasted India's Laxman Shivaramakrishnan out of Test cricket in 1985, and how he punctured Abdul Qadir's confidence in six Tests the following year. Ranatunga's record against Warne is also sound. Allan Border had to dispatch a string of men to the deep when a fearless Ranatunga scored 127 against an admittedly inexperienced Warne at Colombo in 1992. Ranatunga drove the ball brilliantly on both sides of the wicket. Against Shane, left-handed Ranatunga hits with the spin over midwicket, a risk he takes quite well. He also has beautifully soft wrists which enable him to play feather glides through the slips. Few players have the touch to deflect the ball as fine as he does ... and he sweeps well. In summary, he has all the shots to cope with whatever ball Warne bowls to him. If it turns into him he hits powerfully towards the on-side—if it turns away he can deflect it.

HANSIE CRONJE (South Africa)
When he first started out against Warnie he swept a lot and got away with a lot. His career path against Shane may have been different had he top-edged the first ball he faced and been caught ... but he didn't. He proceeded to play well and put just as much pressure on Shane as Shane put on him. Hansie got his confidence up against Shane by lofting him over midwicket in the limited overs game in 1993–94 on perfect batting wickets, and that gave him confidence which ran—for a short time at least—into the Test series.

GRAHAM GOOCH (England)

He has had some epic battles with Warnie. Much has been made of how well he has played Shane but it must be noted he's snared Gooch's wicket six times at Test level, making Gooch, with fellow Englishmen Alec Stewart, Mike Atherton and Graham Thorpe, Warne's most prolific wicket. Gooch is a nerveless batsman who didn't appear to be gripped by any paranoia when facing Shane. Unlike his English team-mates, Graham was always prepared to play the sweep shot leg-spinners hate. I felt Shane bowled too straight at him, for he would continually pad the ball away until he got a really bad ball which he would sweep or belt away. He was a fine player. We should have bowled wider of off-stump where he always looked likely to get an edge behind.

SALIM MALIK (Pakistan)

He must be included in this list for his productive series against Australia in the controversial 1994 series when Warne failed to get him out. I still believe he is yet to face Warne at his best, because Shane hasn't given him a dose of the savage turning leggies that he conjured up in England in 1993. But it must be said Malik, a part-time leg-spinner, can read Warne well and despite a modest series on Australian soil in 1995–96 he remains a fine player of slow bowling. Malik's ability to play leg-spin was enhanced by the fact that he spent 14 years in the same first class and Test sides as Qadir.

And the long list of those who struggle would be headed by:

ROBIN SMITH (England)

His body language portrays his anxiety when facing Shane. He normally talks a lot, saying, "C'mon, watch the ball, watch the ball" and runs on the spot. But when Warne comes on, he'll either say nothing to himself or will gee himself up as if he's about to face a fast bowler rather than a spinner. I can't believe a bloke with Smith's ability can't face a spinner. He had a very defeatist attitude to Shane in the 1993 series. He conceded to me privately early in the series that he had no idea what Shane was up to and I think he virtually wrote off his chances for the series. Perhaps he could have worked harder.

DARYLL CULLINAN (South Africa)

Whenever Cullinan came to the wicket against us, AB used to yell out, "Warm up please, Shane." He could do nothing right against Shane. At one stage he sledged Warnie after he hit a boundary, but he was out a few balls later and Warnie sent him off with the message that it was time to go and look at a few more videos. The only humility Cullinan has displayed in discussing his dealings with Shane came at a guest speaking night in Australia when he was asked what he thought of Warne's flipper, the ball that ruined his tour of Australia. "I don't know ... I haven't managed to spot one yet," he said.

LARRIKINS
OF CRICKET

"When the heroes go off stage, the clowns come on."
HENRICK HEINE

A famous old saying decrees professional sport is not a matter of life and death ... it's much more serious than that.

Sad to say it but there are times when these words seem to ring true. For the fun game it is meant to be cricket can occasionally grow a grim face in the form of an extended form lapse personally or to the side, or simply the pressure that can grind you down throughout a seemingly endless summer.

It is for this reason that I have grown to greatly appreciate the humour in cricket and the fun-loving souls who generate it.

And it is also partly for this reason that I still rate Merv Hughes the most enjoyable team-mate I have had in a decade of first class cricket. Merv had it all, from subtle one-liners to Three Stooges style buffoonery.

Some of his lines were quite clever.

I remember once when Allan Border tried to cajole him back into form he gave the big fellow the following advice.

"When you are bowling why don't you try looking at a place just short of a length outside off-stump."

Merv replied, "What for? I never bowl there."

On another occasion Merv was out early slogging a rank full toss down the ground from Tim May in a Sheffield Shield match at the MCG after being given instructions to go in and get settled before opening up.

Upon his return to the dressing room Merv was greeted by a less-than-impressed skipper Simon O'Donnell, who shouted, "What do you think you were doing?"

Merv interjected with, "What ... you've never got a good one early."

Merv now tells audiences on the guest speaking circuit, "... and now I want to talk about Shane Warne, the man who cost me my career."

This always ensures an immediate and gripping silence before Merv continues with, "... he was told to lose weight ... and did."

Two of the hardest men you'll ever see ... I liked the look of an African tribal mask. That's me on the right!

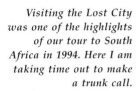

Visiting the Lost City was one of the highlights of our tour to South Africa in 1994. Here I am taking time out to make a trunk call.

The obvious insinuation there being that Merv was told to lose weight ... and didn't.

One of Merv's big lines about his opponents is, "Don't these blokes ever watch tele?"

Towards the end of his career his big shot was the hook which he used with increasing regularity.

If he scored a few runs from the hook one day he would often say to the other batsman, "This bloke obviously hasn't got a telly in his motel room ... fancy bowling there to me."

As so often happens in this type of situation fate intervenes to ensure he is out a few balls later, but it doesn't worry him because he's got his line in.

I give Boonie great wraps for possessing the same reserved body language regardless of whether he's well or badly, and for refusing to let opponents know what his inner thoughts are.

But there was one time when David did drop his mask. He went into the men's toilet at a restaurant in Manchester in 1993 and was staring ahead at the wall when a fellow of similar height with tight, black hair came in and stood at the urinal beside him.

The dry-witted Boon, with his face of stone, didn't even have to look sideways to sense it was Tim May.

The fact that Boon did not acknowledge May's presence enhanced the effect of a small practical joke as he dropped down his right hand to tickle May's private parts.

It was quite a laugh ... particularly since the person standing next to him wasn't May. He wasn't even Australian. In fact David didn't even know him. He looked vaguely similar to May and had a similar coloured shirt on, but that was as far as the resemblance went.

Boonie was horrified ... the man of stone went to water and emerged from the toilets slightly pale-faced.

This story has become slightly enhanced over the years and I have heard an extended version of it that claims the fellow standing next to Boon responded to David's apology, in an effeminate tone, "That's okay ... big fella," before winking and sashaying off.

Another favourite Boon story pertains to our celebration after winning the Second Test against South Africa at Newlands in 1994. It was quite a night and most of us packed our bags before the victory party. But Boonie decided he'd pack later ... a poor move.

He returned from celebrations in a dishevelled but determined manner, somehow managed to pack and was carrying his bags towards reception when a wide-eyed concierge officer started racing towards him.

"I'll take those," he said.

Boonie, with a bag on each side stabilising his wobbly advance, rejected his approach.

Growing increasingly agitated, the concierge offered again but was immediately turned down. Finally he decided it was time to state the plain facts. "But Mr Boon ... you're naked."

Sometimes the things which amuse me most are pure slapstick.

Bob Simpson has always felt strongly about players abusing their equipment when they feel angry.

So Paul Reiffel got a mild dressing down during the '93 Ashes tour when we played Surrey.

Paul was disappointed with his dismissal and threw his bat down with some force when he entered the dressing room after making a duck.

Simmo saw this and said, "You don't need to be showing people you're upset ... you should be naturally upset anyway."

Shane Warne was at the crease at the time, so he hadn't heard Simmo's spiel and was furious with himself for getting out soon after. He was swearing and cursing, so in went moral guardian Simmo to put the core back in decorum yet again.

Just as he was about to pound the pulpit Warne threw his bat towards his coffin.

And then, in a priceless piece of unfortunate timing, the bat rebounded from the coffin and headed like a wooden missile into Simmo's bung knee.

Simmo went off like a cheap alarm clock. "That's bloody stupid Shane," he hollered.

Well, didn't the boys enjoy that one. Particularly since Simmo is one of those blokes you can never get anything on.

Tossing equipment is never to be condoned, though I do recall times when it provided more black humour during the same Ashes tour.

Michael Slater was upset over his dismissal against Kent and threw his pad in the room only for it to ricochet into Steve Waugh, preparing to go in next, who angrily threw it away and then it struck me. At one point all three of us were shouting abuse at each other ... cricketers are hopeless sometimes.

South African allrounder Brian McMillan is a strong-willed character whose hard-nosed approach draws respect from the Australian side. On South Africa's tour of Australia in 1993–94, we started to refer to McMillan as Gerard Depardeau, because he's a dead ringer for the French actor.

Warnie kept it going nicely in the field in the Adelaide Test until McMillan decided he had had enough. After the Test we were scheduled to fly to South Africa immediately for another Test series and McMillan sent the following note to Shane in our room.

It read: "Hey Warne, hundreds of people go missing every day in South Africa, one more won't make any difference."

New chums are inevitable targets on sporting tours. Queensland fast bowler Scott Williams was as green as Tully grass in his first Sheffield Shield trip to Hobart.

When he arrived in Hobart, Williams quizzed the locals about the nuances of the TBA Ground.

He cursed their limited knowledge of their home town, for no-one seemed to know precisely where the TBA Ground was. Finally it was explained to Scott that TBA meant "To Be Announced".

On his first tour Scott was all eyes, ears and questions. He asked if we paid for breakfast or whether it was included in the deal paid by for the association. He also asked whether or not he should make his bed.

May is a natural humourist with an acidic dry wit. On the 1993 Ashes tour, during a low-key tour game at Durham (or as low key as a tour game can be when Ian Botham announces his retirement in the middle of it), May kept leaving tickets for mysteriously named patrons at the front gate.

At the end of each day the poor old gate keeper, who had no idea what was happening, would return the tickets to Tim saying, "Sorry lad, but Mr Del Uge never turned up, neither did Mr F (Flash) Flood or Mr R L (Rather Large) Downpour."

I am not trying to make this chapter the Merv Hughes Life Story, but things happen to Mervyn that happen to no other cricketer.

Merv's eating habits are legendary in the Australian side. The man with a mouth wide enough to contain an entire bucket of McDonald's chips is credited with being a partner in the greatest eating frenzy in Australian cricket.

It was at a Kentucky Fried Chicken outlet in Barbados and I understand the locals still talk about it in revered terms. They rate it the chicken-eating equivalent of Brian Lara's run-scoring records.

Hughes and Craig McDermott entered the shop and decided to order a bucket of chicken. My first reaction was that a bucket in Barbados must not be the same size as a bucket in Australia, which I knew could feed a large family and have a few pieces left over for the kids' lunch and the pet cattle dog the next day.

But no, a bucket was 21 pieces. They also had a large thick shake and a large chips each and, in a welcome concession to good health, a large coleslaw.

The lions and the Christians had nothing on these two. It was terrible to watch. There was chicken going everywhere.

Somehow they got through it and then went back for a large Coke each!

Eating is serious business for Merv. I remember once in the dressing room in Barbados we were approaching lunch and Merv was having a kip on a pile of gear, keeping half an eye on the game but basically relaxing.

Someone mentioned it was five minutes to lunch and up he bounded. So keen was he for lunch that he actually warmed up for the occasion, stretching his legs and loosening his upper body muscles.

The funny thing is Merv wouldn't think about warming up before he batted … but lunch is a much more serious affair.

Merv used to wear these big, old fashioned basketball shoes that looked as if they were 10 years old. They were the type of old fashioned clodhoppers that the Brisbane Bullets basketball side wore in the late 1970s.

Merv is the sort of guy who will get free gear from Puma yet still wear his daggy old favourites.

I had had quite enough of the sight and smell of them during the 1991 West Indian tour and just to make the point I dropped them over the balcony at the team hotel in Antigua into the courtyard below.

It was no big deal. Merv thought he would let them sit there and get them

A Merv Hughes' fitness test in South Afrcia in 1994. The 'big fella' had a bad knee, and to show it was okay had pulled up his shorts—to about his chest!

an hour or so later.

But our thoughts became sidetracked and we went to a nearby casino that night where Merv's eyes suddenly bulged when he saw what looked to be a weathered old sailor walking past in his shoes!

We weren't sure what to do. How embarrassing would it have been if Merv had asked for his shoes back but the man said they were his.

The last thing we needed was a "MERV HUGHES STEALS SHOES OFF POOR OLD TRAMP" headline, so we said nothing.

I am still surprised, not that the old fella found the shoes, but that he was let into the casino wearing them.

On-field banter can also tickle the ribs, sometimes quite intentionally. In a touring game in South Africa in 1994 a local side made a last minute substitution, with the 12th man coming into the team after a batsman had withdrawn due to illness.

Paul Reiffel beat the young substitute four times in a row before finally deciding enough was enough. He said, "You should have stayed as the drink waiter, mate."

Quite affronted, the youngster piped up with, "Who were you expecting as 12th man, Don Bradman?"

I used to do a routine of bowling impersonations which was most enjoyable when we had some highly distinctive bowling styles in the side.

Peter Taylor, with his bouncing approach to the wicket, but most particularly his intense facial expressions that were part of his give-it-all demeanour, was a favourite, along with Merv, Terry Alderman and Abdul Qadir.

Merv starts his run-up with short steps before saving the final call on muscle and tissue until the last few steps. His head bobs around as if there is something loose which, of course, will surprise absolutely no-one.

Once at the Gabba, during a limited-overs match against NSW, I was impersonating a leg-spinner when the ground announcer explained, "This is either Trevor Hohns or Abdul Qadir."

The batsman hit the ball for orbital six and over the PA system came the words, "It's definitely Trevor Hohns."

The bowlers these days are generally a fairly boring, undistinctive lot. With Alderman, Qadir, Taylor and Malcolm Marshall off the scene I'm feeling as uninspired as Queensland cartoonists were the day Sir Joh Bjelke-Petersen left politics.

Life goes on but it is just not the same.

Richie Benaud is another character who deserves mentioning here.

I haven't had a lot to do with him and that is one of the reasons why, at a pre-season launch in Perth, I asked him if he'd be keen to have dinner with Warne, May and myself if I could organise it.

He said he'd love to, "But you must ask permission of your coach first."

Apparently this was how things were done in the old days and I was most impressed by this splash of old world tradition.

Simmo had no problems with it, so the three of us took Richie to an Italian restaurant and enjoyed what remains one of my favourites dinners on tour. Richie, speaking in that clipped, precise style that is all his own, was just a classic.

Amid confessions that we were trying to reduce our alcohol intake we asked him whether he drank much in his day.

Replying in his considered, authoritative way he said, "Never drank much as a young bloke. Never drank until a Test at Nottingham. Made none and three and went to a party that night and was pretty upset, as a guy who made none and three should be.

"My captain, Mr Hassett asked me what I drank and I said I didn't. He said, 'Benaud, you are with me tonight.' He gave me a double scotch and I said it was a bit strong. Then he gave me a single scotch and water and I said it tasted like water.

"So he said to me that a single scotch on the rocks was my drink. I had 11 of them that night and have had a bloody good time ever since."

The moral of the night for me was that cricket hasn't changed much over the years.

One of the most satisfying forms of humour is the old-fashioned Aussie gee-up.

During the last West Indian tour young Ricky Ponting withdrew from a tour match against President's XI on the morning of the game because of an upset stomach after a dodgy bowl of fish chowder the night before.

That meant Mark Waugh had to play and 'Junior' whinged all day about missing out on a precious break and playing in arguably the most boring game of the season. This game was so low key that the most memorable performance of the match came from a herd of goats who stormed onto the playing field during the Australian innings.

Ricky did, however, have just enough strength to come to our team barbecue at the end of the first day, which further heightened Mark's anguish.

Sensing Junior's deep feelings on the matter, the boys decide to torment him further. Ricky wasn't drinking but someone who went to the toilet asked him to hold their stubby to give the impression that he had settled in for a night on the booze.

He disappeared back to bed soon enough and when Mark asked where he had gone someone replied, "He's out on the town."

"Unbelievable," said Junior.

On the final morning of the match someone asked where Ricky had gone and the answer came, "Golf."

The funny thing was he had!

It is time to honour the characters of the game by putting them together in a side which would have won a few matches but, most importantly, been great value to tour with.

MY CHARACTERS OF CRICKET XI

JOHN WRIGHT

The long serving New Zealand batting linchpin was the most humble of Test cricketers. Sometimes when he batted laboriously in a session, which he often did, he would say, "Sorry fellas," to our team as he walked off.

He also said things like, "I just love you Aussies—when you blokes win the series against us tomorrow I wouldn't mind coming to the party. You blokes are tremendous."

We would say, "Shut up, Wrighty," and sure enough next day he would go out and block your path for five hours scoring a century.

If a fly flew past the sight screen Wrighty's concentration would be thrown out of kilter and he would back away from the crease. I'm sure one in every five spectators in Australia has at some stage been moved from behind the sight screen by John Wright.

He used to drive AB crazy by regularly backing away. We'd be giving him heaps and he'd turn around and say, "Sorry Allan, sorry guys ... it's just that for me to be any sort of chance everything has to be perfect."

Renowned for being among the game's most patient players, Wright was dismissed for 71 against us in his last Test, run out by one centimetre on the word of a video umpire.

Wright's last words at his final press conference were, "I really thought I was in but that electronic eye thing gave me out. It's a funny thing that device. They even come into the dressing room and give you a ticket. I didn't know what it was for but I had an idea it wasn't for speeding."

DESMOND HAYNES

He was a great gee-up man for the West Indies who used to fire up his own attack by getting under their skin. Fielding at short leg, he once heard Allan Border call Joel Garner a "big c---" beneath his breath. Desi rushed up to the bowler and shrewdly changed the message to tell Garner that Border had called him a "black c---", which made Joel put the pedal through the floor.

He's also a fine player and the West Indies have not been the same since he retired.

DEAN JONES

A master of the theatrical side of cricket right down to his final dramatic gesture for the Victorian side last summer when he dumped his Victorian sweater and cap in the bin after his side defeated Queensland in the last match of the season. He was a fellow I warmed to greatly. At first he came across as a fairly self-possessed character, but on the 1989 Ashes tour he was my Test match room-mate and I saw a different, caring side to him.

Every team needs a Deano, the up-front, gee-up man. He was a curiously tangential thinker who had a razor sharp mind for the game's peripheral issues whether it be statistics, reporting Keith Arthurton for having a bat which was too wide or asking Curtly Ambrose to take his white sweat bands off.

I could never work out whether he was trying to be controversial taking such action or whether he was doing it to bring justice to the game. That, I guess is Deano, an enigma to the end.

He was full of original ideas on the game. A representative on Victoria's cricket committee, of which Jones was a member, told me Dean would come up with 20 original ideas a summer. The committee might consider 15 out of left-field and discard them but the other five would be excellent and would duly be implemented.

JAVED MIANDAD

At the 1996 World Cup he retired from cricket with the statement, "There's no more characters left in the game—I might as well get out as well."

Javed is not well liked by his opponents, but my feelings about him mellowed after hearing Ian Chappell talking about him during the 1992 World Cup. He said he admired Javed's shrewdness and that his scallywag demeanour was carefully constructed to get under his opponents' skin.

New Zealand 'keeper Ian Smith once said, "Nice day," to Javed during a quiet moment at the crease. Javed replied, "Yes, it's a nice day for the beach, which is where you boys will wish you had been after I am finished with you."

DAVID GOWER

I rate him as a slightly misunderstood character, in that he was a much more committed cricketer than he appeared to be. But there were many moments during his career when his whimsical sense of humour added some levity to what has become a very serious profession.

Gower was spotted drinking a glass of champagne during lunch on the second day of the famous Trent Bridge Test of 1989. Geoff Marsh and Mark Taylor had batted through the first day and we did not lose our first wicket until Swampy fell when the total was 329 on the second morning. There were no other wickets before lunch.

When asked by an Australian player why he was drinking champagne at the break, Gower said, "I'm celebrating our wicket."

During one spirited media debate about the merits of his captaincy Gower had a t-shirt made up saying "I'm in Charge" and 10 others saying "I'm not" which he gave to his troops. A few weeks later he was sacked, so he swapped t-shirts with the new skipper, Mike Gatting.

IAN BOTHAM

I played with 'Both' in his sole season for Queensland and found him most inspiring. If a side was 3–280 at 2.45pm he made you believe they would be all out by 3.30pm.

He was the most positive character you could ever wish to play with. We often batted together and there was nothing more humiliating than seeing half the crowd walk out when he was dismissed.

He single-handedly lifted Queensland's home crowds from beneath 20 000 for five home games to above 60 000 in his one season.

On tour he was accompanied by a minder Andy Withers who would make his special meals, do his laundry and generally look after the small things in life. If he was pestered by some-one Both would call out "Withers" and Andy would rumble in to politely ask the intruder to give Both some space.

He was a generous character. The night before he left for England he had a barbecue, where he gave away presents to all the Queensland players.

Glenn Trimble was given one of Botham's bats and soon after hit what he reckoned was one of the most extraordinary shots of his career—a flat-batted straight six which went no higher than the bowler's head but carried over the boundary line at Brisbane's Norman Gray Oval.

JACK RUSSELL

I like him as a character and mild eccentric. Jack likes his cup of tea with lemon at drinks and team-mates often chide him for spending his life bottled up in his motel room. But he is good company and lives for his cricket.

We get along extremely well and occasionally swap faxes and one-day shirts.

MERV HUGHES

I have made Merv captain of my Characters XI, for he remains the player I've most enjoyed throughout my cricket career. He had a humorous perspective for every occasion. Even when he and Mark Taylor were struggling to get a game in the 1992 World Cup Merv christened himself Kon and Mark Tiki, as they became the Kontiki brothers on a fully sponsored holiday tour of Australia and New Zealand.

The boys had a memorable joke at Merv's expense when he was injured and out of action for the Third Test against New Zealand at Brisbane in 1993. Channel Nine signed him as a guest commentator but instead of just being old-fashioned Merv, he slipped into a commentary mode, where he suddenly became Mr Serious, like Richie Benaud with a moustache.

The boys normally watch the television with the sound down in the dressing room, but this day we turned it up to hear how Merv went in his debut.

We noticed Merv had a peculiar penchant for saying "very".

If someone hit a nice shot it would be a "very" nice shot. If someone hit one of the shots of the session it was a "very, very" good shot. And when Steve Waugh hit a blazing back foot cover drive, Merv called it a "very, very, very" nice stroke.

So we sent a message up to Merv praising him for doing a "very" good job and adding we thought he would become "very, very" accomplished at it, and if Channel Nine signed him up on a long term basis it would be a "very, very, very, very, very" shrewd move.

The message jolted him and instantly he stopped saying "very". The trouble was, he was so used to saying it he suddenly became verbally constipated.

He would say, "... and that's a ve .... a er, ... quite a, um ..."

Ian Chappell would jump in and say "good shot" and Merv would burst back in with "exactly".

TIM MAY

The man with the sharpest tongue in Australian cricket once noted that "bombs are just like cricket ... they are great levellers". This is typical May humour. Maysie once wrote to South Australian Cricket Association chief executive Barry Gibbs requesting that the South Australians be called the (SACA) Spuds.

DANNY MORRISON

People think of him as a down-the-middle type but don't be fooled. If there is ever a cricketing version of *One Flew Over the Cuckoo's Nest* expect Danny to play the lead role. One day Danny will talk to you a lot, the next day he won't say a word, but he is a tremendous bloke and most under-rated bowler.

Danny is the only cricketer I have ever heard confess to throwing a ball on the cricket field.

I remember watching as he bowled a particularly quick ball to Steve Waugh and as he walked back past the umpire he said, "Sorry umpie, I chucked that one ... I got a bit of elbow in it."

I'm not sure whether he was joking or not. Bowlers can feel when they throw a ball. Perhaps he did it on purpose. Or was he pulling the leg?

In a Perth Test match he once deliberately head-butted a short ball from Carl Rackemann, reducing us to an attack of the giggles. I just happened to hear his conversation with the batsman at the other end a few balls later, when he said, "I just wanted to make the point that he wasn't going to intimidate me."

Intimidate me? I can think of better ways of making the point than getting mild concussion.

CARL RACKEMANN

One of the great raconteurs of Australian cricket and one of my favourite characters, Carl's stories just go on and on. One favourite which kept the boys entertained on the 1995 West Indian tour was his tale of how to become an Australian cricket manager. It goes for about 20 minutes and starts out something like, "You are playing third grade for your club and one day, after staying for a drink you are last to leave so you are given the keys to the clubhouse."

So after keeping the keys one week some-one gets the bright idea to make you club secretary. The story goes on and on as the third grader works his way up through the administrative network of his club, State and country.

The boys loved it but you have to be a cricketer to fully appreciate it. I remember one of the player's wives listening to it and having absolutely no idea or great interest in what Carl was talking about.

But once he starts on a big story not even a French nuclear test on the chair beside him can stop Carl from finishing it. An audience of one, no matter how disinterested, is always a quorum for big Carl. And even if that person heads off in the middle of it Carl will happily punch it through for the benefit of the empty chair.

I have a photo of Carl taken on the 1989 Ashes tour in which I have dubbed him 'Paleface Adios', for he reminded me of an old warhorse pacer in his lycra pants with both ankles and one knee strapped.

Carl was a late recruit on the '95 West Indian tour and his selection was warmly received by the likes of Boon, Steve Waugh and myself, as we all enjoy his company.

I smile at the memory of Carl's words at the Pegasus Hotel in Jamaica the night before our last Test.

Carl appeared in the bar and, looking quite businesslike, tapped our physio Errol Alcott on the shoulder and pulled him aside.

The conversation went:

Carl: "Reiffel ... fit?"

Alcott: "Yep."

Carl: "McGrath ... fit?"

Alcott: "Yep."

Carl: "Julian ... fit?"

Alcott: "Yep."

Carl: "Thank you ..."

With the final response confirming all bowlers were fit and Carl would not be needed, the big fellow spun on his heel, ordered two beers and didn't move for the next three hours, knowing that he would not have to bowl again in the West Indies.

It was his quaint and deliberate way of signing off from international cricket forever, but those who played with him will never forget him.

That Miss! *Another great piece of bowling by Warnie, but another time, another place—Karachi, 1994—and I miss the stumping chance that would have given Australia an historic Test win over Pakistan. The batsman was Inzamam Ul Haq. His partner, Mushtaq Ahmed kissed the pitch; I felt like kicking the helmet!*

Previous page: That Ball! *It was Shane Warne's first ball in a Test in England, the First Test at Old Trafford in 1993. Mike Gatting probably still has nightmares about it, too. It pitched outside leg, and turned big, zipping past the outside edge of Gatting's bat and flicking the off stump. As close to the perfect leg-spinner as you'll ever see.*

*A darker moment in South Africa. This was the incident where Shane Warne bagged
Andrew Hudson in the Jo'burg Test, resulting in a heavy fine. There was a lot of pressure
on Warne at the time.*

Opposite page, top: *Who said being a wicket-keeper is easy? South Africa's Gary Kirsten
was all arms and legs when he was called on to 'keep to Paul Adams, the left-arm spinner
with the whirlybird action—and Jonty Rhodes couldn't wait to tell Warnie and me all
about it when we met up at the World Cup.*

Opposite page, bottom: *Not the real David Boon, but Boonie's off-field reputation had
definitely preceded him to South Africa when we toured there in 1994. This zany supporter
rolled up to the Test in Cape Town, his ample, rounded frame "nourished" by intravenous
drip from the contents of the two beer cans fixed to his helmet.*

Previous pages: *That Sting! Mind games were in play at the SCG in the Third Test of
the 1995-96 series against Pakistan when Shane Warne bowled Basit Ali around his legs,
a memorable dismissal because it was planned, and precisely executed—and it was the
very last ball of the day.*

Warnie, doing his thing—and I've got the best view in the house.

THE BOY
CAN PLAY

*"When I was a small kid we used to play ball—day after day
with no trophies, no fans, no bands and no external pressures ...
and we loved it."*

GARY SHAW, AMERICAN FOOTBALLER

The central Queensland township of Biloela, 150 kilometres from Rock-hampton, is known as The Biggest Little Town in the West. As ambiguous as it sounds it's probably a fair description. With a population of 5000 it's no metropolis but it is something more than a fly's footprint on the map of outback Queensland, and any attempts to describe it as such have been thoroughly shot down by the local townsfolk.

A few years ago a Brisbane newspaper wrote an editorial about country policemen having the "misfortune" to be posted to landlocked way-out places like Biloela. Within days it received a letter from 10 out of the 12 policemen stationed there saying, "We actually asked to be posted here."

I knew how they felt. But there have been times when I've had to defend my standing with the people from the township that was my boyhood home. In 1989 a journalist from the Sydney *Sunday Telegraph* interviewed me about life in Biloela, and I confessed, "All there is to do there as a kid is play sport and then when you are old enough you end up drinking with the boys in the pub." Just as a throwaway line I told him that my father's transfer back to Brisbane with the ANZ Bank when I was 17 was probably the best thing that happened to me.

What I was explaining was that the Biloela years were, as they say, part of life's rich tapestry. I used to wear my sister's hand-me-down clothes, a pair of flared jeans which luckily covered my shoes, burgundy platforms. Sometimes I wore short-sleeved polyester shirts and a bead necklace—odd choices you might think for someone who two decades later would be running a fashion business. Going to the drive-in theatre presented the same challenge as anywhere else in Australia: smuggling in stubbies, and smuggling in a few friends under a blanket. The local disco pulsated to the sounds of Hush and Kiss and Peter Allan was pounding out "I Go to Rio". And, once at least, a bottle of Bodega, at the bargain price of $1.99, meant going home to a room that would suddenly start spinning on its axis.

So, you can imagine I almost crashed into my cornflakes that Sunday morning when I saw the headline: "I Almost Wasted My Life On Booze"— says Ian Healy.

I was deeply concerned at the ramifications the story could have in my old home town; the last thing I wanted to do was offend the Biloela townsfolk and it cut me deeply to hear rumbles that they were none too impressed. I sent them my Test wicket-keeping pads for an auction held to raise money for two silos the township had secured from the 1988 Expo site.

My Australian team-mates, particularly Steve Waugh, had no sympathy for me; knowing how sensitive I was about the issue, Waugh tagged me with the quaint nickname, 'Pisstank'.

My dad Nev was an ANZ bank manager and, in March 1972 at the wheel of the family Kingswood, he took the Healy tribe, Mum, me, aged eight, sister Kim and brothers Greg and Kenny to Biloela—a seven hour drive from Brisbane up through Monto and along the Callide Valley past the corn and lucerne crops, to a life of great fulfilment and opportunity.

Our family spent eight years in Biloela and though it is impossible to compare childhoods because you only grow up once, I would never have wanted to be anywhere else.

Biloela provided me with what I felt was the ultimate childhood ... everything I needed in life was literally at the doorstep.

We lived three doors from the high school and opposite the primary school. Mum and Dad trained us to do well at school as well as sport. Cricket and rugby league fields, tennis and basketball courts were a punt kick away. Paradise.

I was always fairly serious about my cricket, but my younger brother Ken, in his early years, was blissfully casual; he was so laid back as a junior he was known to field in the deep with a can of Coke in one hand and a packet of chips in the other.

Dad was occasionally the umpire and when the ball went to Ken Dad would shake his head as Ken juggled his priorities and the occasional packet of chips as he freed a hand to pick up the ball.

We lived on Biloela's main road—Gladstone Road—and Ken and his mates developed a fascination with the giant trucks and petrol tankers that thundered past our brick home. Ken could tell a Kenworth from a Ford or a Mack long before he could pick a wrong 'un from a top-spinner. He and his mates used to stand in our front yard and when a big lorry rumbled past, they would pull their hands up and down in an attempt to prompt the truck driver into blowing his mighty air horn, which would numb the ear drums.

Above: *Cricket in our blood,
with my brother Ken.*

Right: *Ready for anything. As
a boy I was quick on the
draw. Some people think that
when it comes to appealing
nothing's changed!*

*Early days, standing up to a young leggie
during an interstate junior carnival.*

As Ken and his mates would cheer wildly when those horns blew, I would shake my head, and think, "Surely there's more to life than that."

Kenny and myself were different in many respects. When our parents gave us pocket money my first inclination was to save it, planning for how I was going to use it, whereas Ken would have a tuck shop blitz and be broke a few days later.

In our many backyard games Ken was one of those blokes who was never out. Occasionally he would storm inside only to be sent back out by Mum, in her sewing room upstairs, to emulate the Peter Burge of the '90s—playing the role of match referee.

We preferred to play with a hard ball and there was a willow tree root on a dangerous length from which the ball would leap and hit the batsman or sail over the back fence. Sometimes it went straight through the kitchen window of the house behind us, which belonged to John Gesler, manager of the Bank of New South Wales, what else?

A great Biloela character was Charlee Marshall who skippered a Biloela schoolboys team against the men in an open competition.

Charlee, a teacher, poet, farmer, part-time breeder of Shetland ponies, and local legend was born in the Great Depression.

He was one of the great manipulators of young umpires. Often he would appeal for an lbw decision, but would then apologise immediately to the umpire before any decision was given, saying, "Sorry ... that was frivolous."

Next ball he might hit the pads again, but wouldn't even bother appealing, all part of his sideshow to convince the umpire that he only appealed when it was out.

Then the third time he struck the pads—even when it was no closer than the first shout—Charlee, erupting like a bush cockatoo, would shriek, *"Now That's Definitely Out!"*

More often than not the decision went his way, and no-one should be surprised that in Brisbane's Country Week carnival Charlee holds the record of seven lbw's in one innings.

From his little house called Poet's Corner in Thangool, he wrote a beautiful book called *I Couldn't Bowl for Laughin,* telling the story of a fictitious country cricketer which, of course, was based around his own experiences.

His dedication in the front of the book read: "This is a memorial to all those cricketers who tried just as hard, overcoming just as many obstacles and gained just as much pleasure from the game without being blessed with the combination of genius, reflex, good fortune which has promoted their famous fellows to the doorsteps of cricketing renown."

The book is laced with some great old yarns and lively poetry including this little gem called "Billy Hughes".

> *I had a frog called "Billy Hughes".*
> *He lived on Bread and Cheese—*
> *He held the most prophetic views*
> *Of life's perplexities.*
> *Life past we shared in some dank pond;*
> *Life present is a joke*
> *How shall we know what lies beyond?*
> *And Billy answered "Croak."*

Playing against men in open competition as a 12-year-old and young teenager is the most well-known aspect of my days at Biloela. After junior cricket on a Saturday morning, I would hop on my dragster bicycle, with its banana seat and high handle bars, and hare around the three local grounds in the afternoon hoping to get a game with the seniors; and I would do it all again on Sunday morning.

I sat in a scorer's shed waiting for the men to come from their properties—and it was always a moment of some excitement if the numbers were down, meaning I would get a start.

Not that it meant I was bursting onto centre stage, for I would bat at No 11 and field from fine leg to fine leg, a marathon, throughout the afternoon.

When I batted the bowlers generally took it easy on me, but there was one memorable occasion when I was given a taste of something a little more intense. I was 26 not out with our team closing in on victory when Baralaba grazier Merv Bidgood—there are so many Bidgood's out in Queensland's west that they can form their own team at Brisbane's Country Week title—let go a bouncer which flew over my head. In retrospect I'm sure Merv, who is a great bloke, wasn't too serious but there was an outcry from my team-mates on the sidelines.

I'm told Merv still remembers that bouncer—joking that he couldn't go too hard because my dad was his bank manager, but, "what was I supposed to do ... we were trying to win the game." And he does make the good point that it did the kids no good at all for the older players to ease up on them.

That bouncer, a bit of gamesmanship and the usual taunts of "C'mon let's get the kid out" toughened my hide. It was good for me. It embodied everything that was good about a young boy playing against men, being tested and baked in an oven a little warmer than schoolboy cricket. It was not the last time in life I would be pitched into battle ahead of schedule.

There were all sorts of characters in those Country Week carnivals. There was one team, a group of Brisbane Grammar Old Boys, who were called the Little Edward XI.

Their creed was that every player had to change his name for the week so that part of his first or last name had Edward in it.

So their batting list would read: Barry Edwards, Edward Smith, Ted Jones, Ed Ward, Bill Edwardson and so on.

During one Country Week carnival playing for Callide Valley I confronted my older brother Greg, who was playing for an Ipswich team and who sledged me relentlessly when I came out to bat.

I made 85 and by the end of the innings the lads had turned their verbal attention to Greg, reminding him that I had scored more runs than he had.

The Healy family are not super close in that we don't go to each other's place regularly for dinner ... but we are spiritually close and are always there if we are needed.

All three of us boys played for the Queensland Under-19 side, Greg being a fine batsman and Ken a left-handed batsman and part-time 'keeper.

At Biloela I took up rugby league, making the Queensland primary schools side as a trouble-shooting halfback. I played with former Queensland State of Origin players Mark Hohn, Peter Jackson and Michael Hagan but I never felt as comfortable locking horns with the big boys from the city as I did in

Boy among men, and I've no doubt the experience stood me well in my developing years.
The team is Callide-Dawson, with my brother Greg on the right in the back row.
Mick Carriage, right, front row, was tragically killed in the Moura mine disaster.

cricket. My Brisbane rugby league rivals just seemed bigger and better than me; it instilled in me an inferiority complex that I never had to carry in junior cricket, where I always felt more confident.

Games against neighbouring towns were rugged; the boys from Moura were often as tough as their coal-mining fathers. They were the divisional team we always had most problems with.

Part of my job in playing junior rugby league for Biloela was to round up a team and it was never easy. The moral I learnt from this exercise was that players who had to be urged into playing would never come through when it really mattered.

I tried to motivate them and would often pound my fist in the in-goal demanding that they "tackle ... or else!" Sometimes the reply would be "get stuffed, this is only Under-12s."

My stock move was the desperate last resort of every schoolboy league halfback. You ran across field linking behind players—the five-eighth and then the centres—making not a solitary centimetre in the hope that when you finally neared the touchline you would be greeted by the glorious sight of an overlap and winger steaming onto the ball like Carl Lewis.

Sometimes it did happen, but mostly it was just the touch judge and me, and wasn't that a nice waste of breath.

My first outing as a "professional" cricketer was at Biloela as a 10-year-old. I was desperate to buy a new cricket bat and had saved a small amount by scavenging bottles as a ball boy for the Lions rugby league club, where I kept one eye on the game and the other on people likely to discard bottles which I could plunder and make five cents on.

Mum knew that I was saving, and one day when we were playing Monto in the Under-11s, she put me on an incentive scheme, offering me five cents a run to 100 and 10 cents a run after that. I made 179, counting the money as I went! The grand payout of $12.90 was a fortune to me and it was a day to remember when I purchased my new blade.

My first major interstate tour was made at the ripe old age of four, long before I moved to Biloela. I had enrolled with the Gap Under-7 soccer team and after a triumphant tour de force throughout the Brisbane competition (we scored 120 goals to two that season) we were sent to Sydney for several interstate games. My mother came as chaperone for me and Timmy Brusasco, three years my senior and the son of future Australian soccer boss Ian, was made my unofficial minder.

The greatest memory I have of that trip is of feeling quite indignant about having to play on a field without lines…no goal-lines or side-lines…nothing.

It seems strange being four years old and spitting the dummy over playing conditions but I remember we weren't happy.

I loved soccer even if the mental side of the game was a touch beyond my preschool intellect. Our coach George Pagan gave us an early peep into the psychological world of modern sport with well explained theories and a blackboard creed, and positive and negative motivation. However it was gobbledygook to me—I had to let it all go through to the 'keeper.

Mum still tells the story of me coming home from one of George's lessons about positive and negative motivation and saying, quite profoundly, "Mum, you have got to think tegative."

It wasn't my only verbal slip. At one soccer carnival in Brisbane years later we encountered a high class team from the North Coast of New South Wales and I reported to my parents that I was most impressed by the team from "Kessarba".

My parents were surprised; they had never heard of the place. Then, weeks later they learnt through another child that the team was actually from Coffs Harbour.

In grade two I was invited to play in the Ashgrove State School's B teams for cricket and soccer against boys five years older.

These days they would call that fast tracking; I wonder whether today's children would be encouraged to do it?

I am often asked to speak to the topic "Junior sport, more about participation than competition". My standard reply is that I am the worst person to talk about this because I thrived on competition.

I hit my first six in that team. It was a scorching swipe over mid-wicket (now one of my favourite one-day shots) and at the time, as it ballooned over the fence at Marist Brothers, Ashgrove, it lodged in my memory bank as a shot of incredible force. Fifteen years later when I went back to the school I was forced to laugh at my overblown sense of bravado when I learnt the boundary was barely 35 metres, but as a boy it seemed a suburb away.

Like all kids I enjoyed a variety of sports. The Gap Under-7s soccer team (top)—I'm left, front—won a trip to Sydney on the strength of its undefeated season; the Biloela Kangaroos Under-9s rugby league team—I've got the ball—was undefeated, too.

A LESSON,
OR TWO

"For every person who wants to teach there are
approximately 30 who don't want to learn—much."

W C SELLAR

One of the greatest and ultimately most rewarding lessons I have learned in life—that patience and self-belief can crash through the brick walls of adversity—came not in the pressurised world of Test cricket but during my dealings with some 14-year-old school children.

After leaving school I did a Teacher's degree, majoring in physical education, at North Brisbane College of Advanced Education, where I learnt, with interest, about body systems, anatomy and nutrition, a nice sprinkling of knowledge for any ambitious young sportsman. If I had my time again I would probably do a degree angled towards pitching me into the business world but at the time the idea of teaching sport appealed to me. I was particularly interested in learning about the psychology of sport, which I knew would broaden my thinking and my horizons as a cricketer.

My first posting as a teacher was to Kingston High School, a no-frills establishment located deep in blue collar heartland 20 minutes south of Brisbane on the road to the Gold Coast. For a young freshman there could have been no more daunting challenge.

It was like a Test debutant coming to the crease against Wasim Akram on a sticky wicket.

Kingston is appropriately named after early settlers Charles and Harriet Kingston, who certainly were prepared to get a little dirt on their hands when they landed there in 1861, cutting timber, growing grapes, making wine, mining coal and initiating the development of a gravel quarry on their spacious property.

They are buried, along with 12 other early settlers in a small graveyard shaded by a grove of eucalypts at the entrance to Kingston High School. Each morning students walk through the front gate past a sign saying "Kingston High School, a thinking caring school." The school crest, emblazoned on the sign, carries the words "Progress with pride."

Yet for the first few months of my teaching life I was the walking anti-thesis of this motto. In fact my personal creed could have been "No progress and punctured pride." The first tangible sign of the massive challenge ahead had been evident in the circumstances in which I was given the job in the first place.

I was to replace a fellow who did it so tough in his first six weeks he suffered a nervous breakdown; the kids had got to him and when I walked in on his timetable I got the feeling the kids confidently expected to make a gibbering mess of me as well. They almost did.

The Year 8s were manageable because they were slightly insecure in their new surroundings and their uncertainty made them receptive to discipline; and the Year 10s had been given a bit of responsibility and were responsive, too; and the Year 11s and 12s were also maturing and generally sound.

But the Year 9s had the potential to transform an ambitious young teacher into a rubber room candidate in one rebellious month.

On Wednesdays—doomsday—I had them twice, early in the morning for a prac-lesson and straight after "big lunch" for theory. So my job was to instruct them about bones and the body just after a lunch break in which they demonstrated a fair disregard for such matters by beating each other to a pulp.

I started teaching them in February and it was August before they learnt anything more than the basic manners I was trying to force-feed them. The first lesson was spent simply teaching them how to walk into a class room.

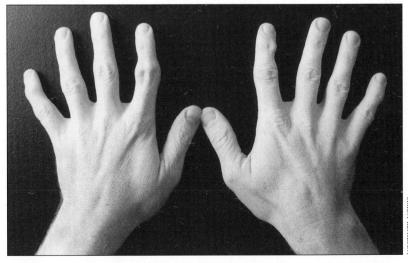

The kids I taught might have been a test of my mettle, but the physical demands on a 'keeper are just as tough. The key to success is persistence. My fingers are a bent mess, but I try to get on the paddock no matter what.

When I'd try to line them up outside the door a fight would inevitably break out. I'd feel like Wallaby Bob McMaster, the referee in World Championship wrestling, as I'd try to sort it out. Just when things would go quiet, just when I thought I had them, there would be pushing and shoving at the back of the line and I'd bellow "I am waiting on you two."

Finally, after endless rehearsals, they would file into the room. But by the time the last stragglers reached the door, act two of the civil war would be well underway inside.

Filled with the dauntless enthusiasm of a new blood, I would stay up all night preparing my lessons for them, and, in what I thought was a shrewd game plan, would try and deviate from the routine teacher's sermons and appeal to their other senses by having overhead transparencies and other graphics.

But it was hopeless. Defeated, I'd often return from class to my subject master, Neil Sivyer who would ask me how I was progressing.

I would throw my gear disconsolately on the desk and snap back "Shocker."

I would say things like, "I have got to test them on things in August, but how can I test them when I haven't taught them anything? But there's no use teaching them anything if they haven't got manners."

I remember being in tears as I drove home to my girlfriend Helen, to whom I poured out my frustration, saying things like, "They are treating me like dirt ... they have no respect for me ... I want to throw it in."

I am pleased to say that I was to develop a great liking for Year 9. They weren't smart alec kids who chipped away at you in a conniving, supercilious, fashion—they were essentially good kids, honest but slightly rebellious.

I remember one saying straight to my face, "Get f---ed" and I snapped back, "No you get f---ed." The reply stunned him and he responded, with some indignation, "You can't say that" and I came back with, "I just did."

Of course, no teacher's textbook advises that sort of borderline conduct, but I was banking on the kid thinking he was tough, and therefore unlikely to report me for fear of being seen as a squib. He said nothing and after that we got along well.

My other questionable piece of off-the-cuff disciplinary work would have earnt me a six week holiday from Ron Coote's Australian Rugby League judiciary. One dewy Friday morning I had sent the kids for a run and one mischievous character was ankle tapping the girls and being a general nuisance, never suspecting I was watching his every move.

As he jogged past me I shot out a hand to grab him, but accidentally skittled him with a "tackle" rugby league players know as a coat-hanger—I caught him on the chin. Horrified at what I had done, I was happy to see no damage had been inflicted, and being a subscriber to the theory that attack is the best form of defence, I teed off with my "If you ever do that again ..." spiel.

*And it all began in Biloela. The Healy clan, with the Sheffield Shield,
the Frank Worrell Trophy ... and AB. We were at a Save The Children charity
dinner. From the left, Helen, Ken, Dad, AB, Mum, Greg, Sandra and me,
Kim and her husband Geoff Boon are kneeling at the front.*

I guess it's true that sometimes you have to be tough on the kids to earn their respect. The fact that they wanted me to stay on as their teacher in later years meant a lot, and while they were always cocky, there were many moments of fulfilment and learning in between. I got the feeling my Year 9 rebels had sorted out early that I wasn't too bad, but they had decided to test me out just for the fun of it.

Before doing my Teacher's degree I had spent a fulfilling senior year at Brisbane State High School—we had left Biloela when I was in Year 11. The Biloela years were great but I felt I was ready for the broader challenge of metropolitan schools, higher intensity sport and a more challenging, competitive life in general.

The GPS cricket season is unusual because it starts in February-March, less than ideal because everyone else in the country is starting to gear up for the football season.

So, at Brisbane, State rugby union provided a fresh and invigorating challenge. I was no speed machine but I could tackle and managed to snaffle a first XV berth at inside centre.

One of my first games, a trip to New Zealand for a trial against an Auckland Grammar side which included Mark Greatbatch, later to play Test cricket with New Zealand, remains an indelible memory for me—I suffered the distressing experience of being trapped at the bottom of a collapsed ruck. Panic-stricken and feeling the need to show some form of aggression, I grabbed hold of the rival hooker's testicles, closed my eyes and squeezed as hard as I could. When I opened my eyes there were just the two of us lying there—and across his face was the look of absolute rage. His swinging fist just grazed my face as I bolted. My next moment of anxiety came after the match—they announced which of the Auckland players' families we were to be billeted with.

I thought, "If I get the hooker I'm swimming home across the Tasman." I got someone else, fortunately.

It's uncanny how names from your junior sport days can keep bobbing up in later life. I still remember well a conversation from my tour of England with the Australian Under-19 team in 1983; five of us were in a London cafe when we wondered who would be the first player from our squad to play first class cricket. Three of the lads nominated Queensland fast bowler Harley Hammelmann; he became a long time member of the Queensland squad and a sound first grade performer, but never did play a first class game. I strongly nominated Craig McDermott but the others questioned whether Craig was mentally robust enough for first class cricket. I felt Craig had been ear-marked for greater things and fast-tracked through the system from the time he first played for Queensland Under-19s as a 16-year-old. Yet even I would not have suspected Craig would advance so quickly he would surge into Test cricket within 18 months of our Under-19 tour. Craig was one of three in our team who played first class cricket the summer following our tour, Mike Veletta and Tony Dodemaide being the others. Another player on that tour was a batsman named Craig Bradley who scored a fine 'Test' century on tour; our eyes spun like lemons in a poker machine when Craig told us the size of a contract he had been offered to play AFL football.

While the rest of us were deciding how we would spend our 20 pound per week allowance, 'Braddles' was checking the prices on a new Mazda RX7. The athletic and multi-talented Bradley had a brief Shield career, but made a much greater impact as a premiership winning star for Carlton.

Though I had won Cricketer of the Carnival at the interstate championships prior to the tour, I missed selection in the first 'Test', but played the last two and fielded at second slip, where I took two catches. I could not prise the top 'keeping spot from New South Wales' solid performer Bronco Djura, who had shone over the stumps to the Blues spinners at the carnival. He was a good 'keeper and a solid batsman, an unusual but strong character who was generally good for the team. He later gave cricket away to play rugby league for South Sydney where he was a regular first grader.

It was on that tour that I first displayed a curious and embarrassing habit of sleepwalking. If we are to be serious about providing a warts and all book, we must reflect on the night at Southampton when we had 10 pints each, a big drink for 18-year-olds.

I was rooming with Craig McDermott, yet when he came into the room I was standing naked, speechless and asleep behind a curtain.

When he asked what I was doing I told him what I thought was the truth: "There's a kangaroo in my bed."

I am not sure what his reaction was, but he somehow managed to cajole me into getting back in bed. Still mentally off with the pixies, I started screaming, "The bloody thing's on my knee ... now it's on my head."

I do something unexplainable like that once a tour and once carried the nickname 'Swahealy' because of the indecipherable babbling I make in my sleep.

Mike 'Waggy' Veletta, who went on to play for Australia, is a great character, tremendous company and a prankster. He was renowned among the boys for wearing really old gear which looked as if it had been purchased at Steptoe and Sons. His cream pants were the old non-stretch cotton style with the zip up the front. He would have a cupboard full of new bats at home, yet he would use the oldest one of the lot.

Waggy was the architect of a great "get" on the 1991 West Indian tour when he was rooming with Steve Waugh. As Steve slept at the Rockley Resort in Barbados, Waggy left a trail of crumbs leading from the balcony with the final one placed on top of Steve's groin in the hope of persuading the small birds who had descended upon the balcony to come inside and have a decent peck.

When I entered Brisbane grade cricket it was at the end of a hard-nosed era of cricketers who were renowned for being quick on the lip. A taste of things to come arrived in my first game in third grade for Norths, against Sandgate-Redcliffe. Graham Dixon, now general manager of Queensland Cricket, asked me from slip whether I had been practising all week in front of the mirror as I battled through the rain at Deagon.

Current Queensland selection chairman Max Walters was another Sandgate man who had a parting shot at me, sending me off one day with the message to "go iron your schoolboy shirt" after I'd worn my Australian Under-19 shirt and failed in first grade.

And I wasn't immune from my own team-mates either! I was fielding at short leg to former Queensland spinner Graham Whyte, and accidentally put my right boot behind the stump line to concede a no-ball for having three men behind square leg. Whitey gave it to me so hard I wished there had been an on-field hole for the fielders helmet, because I felt small enough to crawl into it.

Greg Ritchie once said that he liked to see a dose of verbal spice in the grade competition, because if you have a marshmallow club scene you get soft cricketers at first class level. And I agree, because if players are hungry there will always be occasional fireworks. But I rate a tough cricketer as more than someone capable of making big noises.

It is interesting to note that in the era when Brisbane grade cricket was allegedly at its combative best, Queensland had the softest side in the Sheffield Shield.

A tough cricketer to me is someone who can cope with any verbal barbs, maintain their concentration and make big runs, and dedicate themselves to playing tough cricket without losing control. I am sure some of those players who were being touted as tough men were actually out of control and it would have done their cricket no good.

To play with the likes of Geoff Dymock, Don Allen, Rob Kerr was great for me. And just as important was the tutelage of the club's senior wicket-keeper Bryan Phelan, who became a trusted mentor and friend.

Fortified by their guidance, it certainly didn't hurt young players like myself to be exposed to this sort of heat. The theory was that it provided a hard-baked exterior by the time we reached first-class level.

CALLED UP

"There is no security on this earth, there is only opportunity."
GENERAL DOUGLAS MACARTHUR

Lorraine Whitney, the motherly former office secretary of the Queensland Cricket Association, had the bubbly tone of any major good news bearer when she rang my office at 3.15pm on 31 March 1988. Lorraine is the warmest of people under any circumstances but this day she was especially chirpy when she asked whether I was aware of the "big news".

I replied in the negative as I pondered what could possibly be big news in the cricket world; the fading embers of the season were being swept away by a torrent of publicity accompanying Brisbane's new football team, the Broncos, who were storming undefeated through the early rounds of their first winter.

Then there was silence on the line while Lorraine handed the phone over to QCA secretary Grantley Evans who announced with an excitable quiver in his voice, "You are in the team."

"Yes ... the Queensland team to play in Kingaroy this weekend," I replied, experiencing the twinge of satisfaction that all rookies feel when their spot is confirmed for the next match, no matter how small the assignment.

"No, the Australian team to tour Pakistan," he said, sending me freefalling into mental Disneyland.

Only those Casket agency people whose job it is to tell people they have "won a motzer" could understand the numbness which descended upon me after hearing those words.

I had received the news at my new work place, Associated Fashion Distributors, and the office secretary, Sandy Ferguson, says she will never forget my reaction. "You just stood up and went as white as a sheet ... I thought there might have been a death in the family. There wasn't much work done that afternoon."

My thoughts were racing. Pakistan? When, where and most importantly, why me?

My knowledge of the tour was so limited I had to ask when it was on.

The only time I had even spoken about the tour was at the airport on the way home from the Sheffield Shield final against Western Australia a week earlier, and that had been to wish valiant left-arm fast bowler Dirk Tazelaar all the best at the selection table. He had bowled exceptionally that season and, in my view, had to be in the selection frame.

But me?

I was only in the Queensland side because regular custodian Peter Anderson had broken a thumb while standing over the stumps to Ian Botham in a Shield match in Perth midway through the season. For all I knew, with Ando back in action the following summer, I might have played my last Shield match, never mind playing for Australia.

I asked Evans who the other 'keeper was in the squad and the reply was another mule kick between the eyes.

"There is no other 'keeper ... you are it."

Grantley read through the team and then, upon request, ran through it a second time, but the exercise was lost on me. I was still thinking about my selection.

No sooner had I put the phone down than I was hauled from the clouds by a work mate who sensed a mischievous hand at work.

"You know it's April Fool's Day tomorrow?"

Of course! Damn them, I thought. I didn't mind a joke but this was in bad taste. What's more they'd got me cold ... and, they seemed so convincing.

The "joke" went a step further when my Queensland team-mate Trevor Hohns rang minutes later to congratulate me.

Because 'Cracker' Hohns had been waiting 13 fruitless first-class years for the phone call from heaven which I had just received I thought that he, of all men, would know just how much such a moment would mean to a battling young cricketer—I just couldn't imagine him tampering with someone's emotions on such an important matter.

And he sounded excited and genuinely pleased for me, but I had suspicion oozing from every pore, so I asked him, "Who put you up to this?"

Cracker, mildly amused by my cynicism, declared and redeclared his sincerity. Starting to feel convinced that I had indeed struck the jackpot, I then phoned my long time best mate Brad Inwood, the former Queensland Sheffield Shield cricketer, to tell him the news.

"Bullshit," was his considered response.

Inwood, like myself, was well-versed in the art of media pranks. Over the years, from our days as teenage rivals and team-mates in central Queensland, a regular gag was for someone to ring up a team-mate and pose as a local pressman.

"Your form has been tremendous, you must be so happy?" was a standard question in relation to a bogus storyline about selectors smiling on you.

Any self-flattering answer such as, "Yes, I feel I'm ready for big things," would be immediately relayed back to the boys for a sure-fire laugh.

Above: *Early success.
It's in the interstate
primary schools
carnival in Brisbane,
1975, and a South
Australian batsman,
Paul Hosie, has
tickled one down the
leg-side.*

Right: *Arriving home
from the Under-15
tour in 1977. They
were held in Perth,
not such a happy
memory for me in
later years. With me
is Peter Boon, suit-
ably built for a fast
bowler. The beads
were fashionable,
I think, but not
necessarily meant to
go with a maroon
warm-up jacket.*

83

I then rang my dad and mum at their work offices separately, opening the conversations with the line, "Are you sitting down?"

One of the satisfying moments in the life of any Test cricketer is telling his parents that a life-long dream has been fulfilled and all those frenzied Saturday morning car rides, pre-season gear buying expeditions, boring trophy nights and backyard tutelage had yielded a green and gold cap.

Pangs of disbelief were still niggling at my elation, however, and I welcomed an offer of "nine holes" from my boss and soon to be brother-in-law Ian Perkins. But I did leave a message at work that I had gone to Brisbane Golf Club and would handle all media enquiries there, even alerting the club barman to be ready for a torrent of calls from the media which I would respond to once my round was over.

The round relaxed me, and I rationalised that the news was true, that I must have been in the Australian team to tour Pakistan. I could have hit a hole in one that afternoon and probably forgotten about it two holes later.

Steeling myself for the media grilling I had been anticipating from about the second hole on, I spent a while freshening up in the downstairs locker room, then bounded up the stairs towards my "new life", and asked the barman for the list of callers.

He said, "There isn't one." I put my head on the bar in whirring disbelief and I pondered the day over a cold beer.

At that stage of my career I was no expert on the media but I knew enough of their workings to know that my Test selection would be big news, footy season and all, particularly in Queensland.

Without a call from the media I could not accept that I was in the side. Surely it had to be an April Fool's joke. Without recognition from the media the whole thing had a surreal air about it. It wasn't the plaudits and headlines I was seeking ... just confirmation of my selection. It was like going down the aisle and not hearing the words "I do."

It was not until years later that this great media riddle was explained to me. Friday was not only April Fool's Day but it was also Good Friday. Many leading newspapers, including my home paper, Brisbane's *The Courier-Mail* didn't publish on Good Friday, so there was no need for them to contact me on Thursday.

Eventually, it was my father who gave me peace of mind; he phoned the QCA and spoke to office staff member Ian Sturgess, who said, "We thought you would have known this morning."

That night I packed for a long-arranged Easter weekend Moreton Island holiday with Craig McDermott.

The press may have been missing in action on Thursday, but by Friday morning I was The Man, besieged by reporters from all four Brisbane television stations; the whole business was a bit overwhelming.

CRAIG SHAW/COURIER-MAIL

Two "big shots" who influenced my career,
Jeff Thomson and particularly Greg Chappell.

Still trying to come to grips with the decision I suddenly started to pull words out which I never use, and from some cobwebbed corner of my sub-conscious I revealed that I "empathised" with those wicket-keepers who were more experienced but who missed the job. A quick check of the dictionary later left me relieved that the meaning of empathy—the power to deeply understand someone else's emotion—was precisely the description of my feelings. Thank goodness!

The selection capped an incredible period of my life in which I snared an enjoyable new job as a fashion salesman for AFD, married Helen Perkins, after a five-year courtship, two weeks after my Test call-up and even fluked a $3000 subsidy for my wedding at a bridal expo at Yeerongpilly.

Somehow Helen and I managed to leave for Moreton that Friday after-noon and the chaos dissipated with a serene two-hour barge ride on the Moreton Venture. As the old vessel gently surged through a slight swell on a perfect autumn day, the thought hit me that my world had just changed forever.

Once the barge hit shore at Tangalooma, McDermott, who had been there for a day or two, loomed up and I broke the news that I would be touring Pakistan with him.

"Bullshit," he said.

I thought, "Don't you start ..."

IAN *!*!*?
WHO?

"Destiny is what you are supposed to achieve.
Fate is what kicks you in the arse to make you do it."
HENRY MILLER

Merv Hughes often tells the story about the day he was driving with Victorian wicket-keeper Michael Dimmatina to the wedding of team-mate Jamie Siddons when their idle chatter was rudely interrupted by stunning news.

Merv and 'Dimma' were en route to Siddons' home town of Robinvale on the Murray River, 80 kilometres upstream from Mildura when a radio news story announced that Ian Healy had been chosen as Australia's wicket-keeper for the tour of Pakistan.

The way Merv tells the story, the conversation stopped, both jaws dropped, they stared at each other in disbelief and said in unison, "Ian f---ing who?"

Both Merv and Dimma had been hoping to make the team but neither had. Dimma looked at Merv and said, "At least you missed out to blokes who have played a bit of cricket (Bruce Reid, McDermott and Tony Dodemaide)."

Dimmatina, quite understandably, was shattered. The controversial decision was a hot topic of conversation among the cricket fraternity at the wedding reception as guests searched for one decent reason why I should have been given the job.

Dimmatina was not the only player to be shattered by the decision. On the night I was selected Peter Anderson, my Queensland squad mate and three years my senior, learnt from a nightly television news bulletin I would be the sixth 'keeper tried at Test level since Rod Marsh retired four years earlier, taking with him a generation of Test match pedigree.

Over the next few weeks there was to be a ring-around of most of the Sheffield Shield 'keepers in Australia to discuss the decision. More than any other cricketing trade, wicket-keeping is a numbers game. Mine had come up, and I am forever grateful.

The whole astonishing turnaround has convinced me that in Australia at any time there could be as many as 12 'keepers who could handle the Test job. The six State 'keepers could do so and somewhere hidden away in grade cricket there would be highly skilled yet unrecognised glovemen who never get the chance even at Shield level.

In media interviews after my selection I had been at pains not to portray myself as starstruck; I shied away from those wide-eyed, debutant lines like "I have been watching these guys on television for a long time ... I can't believe I will be playing with them."

But beneath that flimsy mask of self-assurance my emotions were quite different. When I first met the remainder of the squad at a pre-season training camp in Brisbane I noted in my daily diaries, with some amazement, "They were just normal blokes."

In many people's eyes, and mine, I was a selection out of left field. In the eyes of some it was so far left field it was as if I had been plucked from the car park.

I had played just six first class games and four planets effectively had to come into line for me to be in the side. They were:

(1) The selectors being unhappy with incumbent Greg Dyer and deciding to drop him.

(2) Anderson having a broken finger.

(3) A pre-season Test tour being scheduled.

(4) The panel, fed up with consistently shuffling the deck, making a collective decision to be patient and give me every possible chance to cement my position.

Extraordinary.

So why me?

It took me about seven years to have the courage to probe for the full story behind my selection. In June, 1995, I was in Jackson's on George Street in Sydney having a beer with a group of players and Greg Chappell was present.

I know selection room secrets are not supposed to be breached, I know Greg respects this code and I accept that my job is to play and not to ponder the whims of the selectors ... but I simply had to ask.

This was Greg's answer.

> *We were looking around for fellows to handle the job for the long term and no-one had stamped themselves as the obvious choice. We had tried a lot of players in different positions after the retirements of several key players and the disruption of the South African rebel tours.*
>
> *The consensus was that we had to focus on the mid- to long term and look for people with the right type of character. Geoff Marsh, David Boon and Allan Border had been the rocks of the side and we needed more people with this type of character to be successful.*

There was nothing more certain than that the vast majority of work in the Tests would be up to the stumps and we felt that we needed someone who would not go to pieces if they made an early mistake.

So we felt that you were a bloke who had limited opportunities and you could 'keep and bat and had a good temperament, someone who would retain a sense of humour in the darkest hour.

People might say that I got you in, but it was a panel decision. I don't deserve the credit. We made a lot of gambles that I was involved in which didn't come off.

In you I saw some of the qualities of Rod Marsh, who was extremely competitive, as strong as an ox, fired up the team and never took an easy option.

I watched you closely in Queensland's match against Tasmania in Launceston in 1988 and felt you detached yourself from the controversial climate of the time pretty well.

If only I had as much confidence in myself at that stage!

When you next park your car near the Australian team hotel don't be alarmed if you hear "plink", "plunk" — it's only me practising in the car park. It's an old trick I learned from Peter Anderson, and it brings rhythm to my game.

As magnanimous as Greg was about my selection being a panel rather than personal choice I feel he understated his decisive hand in the matter.

He simply had to be the driving force behind my inclusion—he was the only selector who knew me. It would be a bold selection panel that chose a rookie on the strength of six first class matches unless one of the selectors could offer some sort of strong endorsement of his character.

That man had to be Chappell.

Greg said he had watched me closely on and off the field during Queensland's 94-run loss against Tasmania in Launceston in February, 1988, which, unbeknown to me at the time, was one of the most important matches of my career.

On the third morning of the game Glenn Trimble and I added 163 in a session as Trimble became the first Queenslander in 11 years to notch a century in a session. He scored 39 runs in the opening half hour while I was scoreless, but I finished 58 not out when we declared 118 behind at lunch in pursuit of the outright win we needed to make to host the final.

As wet behind the ears as I was in that Shield summer I still remember sensing Greg was on the lookout for something special during his visit to Tasmania ... and it wasn't apples or Boag's beer.

I recall at lunch on the third day watching AB and Greg talking in the corridor outside the dressing room. Within 15 minutes of their conversation Allan announced we would declare immediately.

After speaking at length with Allan, Greg must have known this would be our decision. He may have even had some input into it.

Yet, quite mysteriously, he then came into our dressing room and meandered nonchalantly over to a corner where I was eating fruit salad with my pads on, unsure of whether I would be 'keeping after lunch or batting on.

"Keep your head down, there's a century for the taking," Chappell said to me.

I replied, "If I start wondering about the century I will stuff things up for sure."

This was my off-the-cuff answer but looking back I reckon Greg knew we were going to declare and he was simply testing my head to see how my temperament was holding up.

When I spoke to Chappell before I left for Pakistan, he gave me great peace of mind by saying, "Think beyond Pakistan."

I believe he wanted me to think of myself as a long-term appointment, a thought which would provide both comfort and a mental spur to me during some dark and testing days ahead.

Apart from giving me the break of a lifetime it was uncanny how Chappell would chime in with a pep-me-up line in his nationally syndicated newspaper column just when I needed it most. I couldn't work out whether it was

*Enjoying a workout with Rod Marsh; it took me a while to break
into the Marsh bank of wicket-keeping knowledge.*

just a coincidence or whether Greg was reading me better than anyone has.

Midway through my first season as Test 'keeper Chappell wrote a column about how nice it was not to hear that depressingly familiar cry of "sack the wicket-keeper" reverberating around the Australian cricket scene.

He praised my temperament. "It must be satisfying for the selectors, with a tour of England just months away, that the one position they don't have to worry about is the 'keeper."

Chappell's part in my selection had been well-documented, not so Allan Border's. Yet I believe he was instrumental in my shock recruitment. I have never spoken to him about this, or barely anyone else for that matter.

When the Australian side returned from their World Cup victory in 1987 and I had played just two first class matches for Queensland, McDermott startled me with an amazing statement at a Maroons net session.

Like people recalling where they were when they learnt of Elvis' death or some other moment that meant a lot to them, I can still see the outline of the sight screen and the Queensland Cricketer's Club behind Craig as he casually mentioned, "AB wants you in the Australian team."

"You're kidding," I said.

It was a most bewildering, yet inspiring moment. When you are a battling fringe player craving selection—for Queensland, never mind Australia —every skerrick of positive feedback is a pep pill for the rugged grind ahead. When it comes from the Australian captain, even via someone else's lips, it is as if someone has slipped a gold bar in your pocket.

It's hard to believe that precisely one year before my selection a story appeared in a Brisbane paper claiming that I was "on a cricket merry-go-round, uncertain of where and when I should get off".

In two of my three years as Queensland Colts captain I had been chosen as a specialist batsman behind Peter 'Ando' Anderson, and I admitted in the article, "I used to be a batsman-'keeper but now, if I am going to bat at No 8 I guess I have to be a 'keeper-batsman."

It was hardly the type of tunnel vision commitment you expect from the country's next Test 'keeper. But these were tempestuous and confusing times. Queensland cricket stalwart Brian Gaskell said to my parents, "Ian really should give 'keeping away and concentrate on becoming a batsman."

I nearly did. It was only the persuasive words of Test selector Greg Chappell and the then Queensland selection chairman Ernie Toovey that cajoled me into keeping on 'keeping. I remember storming into my parents' place at Sunnybank Hills a year or two before my Queensland selection after a poor club game and saying with total exasperation, "That's it ... I'm quitting. I have had enough. I don't know why I even bother putting in all the effort I do. I am never going to get anywhere."

It was a classic case of the back-up-'keeper blues all reserve glovemen have suffered since Adam kept wicket in a pair of bamboo pads.

My younger brother Ken, himself a batsman-'keeper who would later learn all about the frustrations of standing in a cricket queue, just sat there watching television without saying anything as I let fly. I am sure he would have "empathised" with my frustration.

Mum, ever the mediator, offered the philosophical words, "Is that what you really want?"

Of course, deep down, it wasn't. I loved the game too much to toss it in.

Reflecting on that incident, Mum says, "We always felt Ian would make it but there were many times when there just didn't look to be an opening. I would never have tried to force him to go on if he didn't really want to. It was just one of those little dramas families go through."

With Anderson entrenched as the State's No 1 'keeper, I was torn between moving interstate, becoming a batting specialist and simply toughing it out in an unsatisfying slipstream.

The three games of first class cricket I played when Ando sustained finger injuries for the first time were a teasing appetiser which fuelled my desire to sink my teeth into the main meal.

At the end of my first summer, I heard second hand that South Australian captain David Hookes had asked for my phone number, for the Crow-eaters were having 'keeping problems. Had he made the call I would have had my bags packed before the end of the STD pips. But the call never came.

Curiously, the only person who tossed my name up as a candidate for the Pakistan tour was an old mate, Darryl Case. When he mentioned it at a barbecue a few weeks before the tour was announced he was given all the attention of a racing pundit tipping a Melbourne Cup winner in June.

After two or three "yeah rights" people resumed their conversations. I understand he still dines out on the story.

Soon after I was chosen for Australia, a shattered Ando declared in *The Courier-Mail* he was teetering on the brink of retirement.

"I don't know whether what has happened is fate, bad luck or politics, but I just don't want to be kept dangling any longer," said Anderson, who had served a seven year apprenticeship under Ray Phillips before finally getting his chance for Queensland.

"Retirement now is a very serious option. I don't think I have any other option. The Australian selectors consider Healy a better cricketer and wicketkeeper than me. That's it. Final. And obviously Healy is going to get better.

"No-one here is too upset about what has happened. Most people think: What the heck, we've got a Queenslander in as 'keeper. What's it matter which one." They were strong, emotional words flowing unrestrained from the heart of a fine player.

I felt deeply sorry for Anderson, if not quite to the point of feeling guilty

I had taken the spot he was craving for. Every 'keeper knows what it is like to be stuck in heavy traffic.

But though my emotions were spinning like a tumble drier I still had the strength not to soften my approach to the job. As unlucky as Ando and the other 'keepers were, if I felt too sorry for them and guilty about being the top dog, within months I would be back in Shield cricket feeling sorry for myself that someone had snatched my job. Under any circumstances the job represented a devilishly tough challenge—to enter it carrying an inferiority or guilt complex would have spelt the end of me.

Anderson was bitter but never at me. From the shattering instant when he first learnt of my selection he remained totally selfless. His support is something I will never forget.

I learnt more from him than from any other wicket-keeper I have seen, spoken to or worked with. The two of us spent hundreds of hours training together at Easts, Colts and at State training where I learned much more from him than he did from me. In my formative years he was the master and I the apprentice.

When I started working with Ando I felt he was a much better 'keeper than me. Ando's fanaticism impressed me deeply. His attention to detail was superb. At that stage I didn't even have a great idea of how I wanted my technique to evolve. I just went out and 'kept.

But because everything he did was so purposeful, I started to think about developing a style and honing it.

Ando is now retired from the game and business interests have kept him away from the Gabba but he still keeps an eye on my 'keeping. "I know his game so well I can tell how well he is 'keeping," he said recently.

The first time Ando and I crossed paths after my selection was at an off-season cricket function at the QCA a month later. Feeling sheepish and down-right uncomfortable about approaching him, I struggled to make eye contact. Sensing this, he made the effort to come up and congratulate me. Once the ice was broken we talked for a long time.

But I was still gripped by a sense of insecurity and mild paranoia.

So highly did I rate Anderson that only months earlier I, and seemingly most other cricket observers around Australia, reasoned he would be Australia's next 'keeper. This pepped my motivation to secure the spot as his Queensland deputy and perhaps snare the number two berth on the 1989 Ashes tour.

At the time of my selection I had not even met the 'keeper I replaced, New South Welshman Greg Dyer. We had a chat in my first season in the national job and I found him most personable.

During the only Sheffield Shield match I played against him a ball bobbled up my arm and he caught it and appealed loudly for the catch. When it was

BARRY PASCOE/COURIER-MAIL

*Peter Anderson, whose misfortune turned out to be my good
fortune. He was the main influence on my career.*

turned down he said to me, "We know Heals, don't we?" but I swear I didn't
hit it.

I still regard the first six Sheffield Shield games for Queensland as the best
games I have played in my life.

I played every match as if it was my last which, quite possibly, it could
have been pending Ando's recovery from finger injuries.

Each night I would have a few drinks and merrily head to bed around
midnight or 1am. The next morning I would clear my head and shake myself down at the team warm-ups and get ready for battle again.

Of course there was pressure involved but the incredibly high level of
enjoyment I derived from these games seemed to over-ride it. It was almost
as if the nerves were washed away by a king tide of adrenalin and pleasant
emotions.

Almost a decade later I still reflect on the moral of those matches ... if you
can convince yourself you are really enjoying what you do you will excel at
it, or at least play the best you can.

It is when something becomes just a job, the enjoyment subsides and life
becomes, at times, dangerously serious.

NO MORE MONKEY

"Patience is a bitter plant but it has sweet fruit."
OLD PROVERB

When the moment came I wasn't sure whether to laugh or cry, to raise my arms in triumph or to pound the table in frustration. Queensland had won the Sheffield Shield at last, but I was a 30-hour plane trip away, on the edge of a small island where the words "Sheffield Shield" represented nothing except possible names for your child in a world where they call their babies anything but the obvious.

I was on the tiny Caribbean island of St Lucia and only a Queenslander would fully understand the depth of my whirling emotion on 28 March 1995 when news of Queensland's first Sheffield Shield win reached me. It was as if the biggest party in the world was happening in my backyard but I had been called into the office. For 60 years Queenslanders had lived with the indignity of never having won the Sheffield Shield, and each year the phobia grew an extra ugly tentacle. Pessimistic old-timers would say, "They'll never win it in my lifetime," and southerners such as David Hookes made the sniping forecast, "They'll never win it this century." By the 1994–95 season it was not so much a monkey that was resting on Queensland's shoulders as King Kong.

Winning the Sheffield Shield meant as much to Queensland as winning the America's Cup in 1983 did to Australia.

Still, if I couldn't attend Queensland's biggest ever sporting party then I decided to do the next best thing; I formed a Sheffield Shield V-day sub-branch and with Queensland cricket writers Jim Tucker and Robert Craddock, who were covering the Australian tour to the Caribbean, I made a beeline for the beach bar of the St Lucia hotel. On the stroke of 8pm we cracked open the bottle of Bundaberg rum the thoughtful Tucker had brought over for this specific purpose and by 2am the next morning, appropriately under a full moon and, with top buttons undone and shirt tails flapping in a warm Caribbean breeze, we were puzzling curious fellow drinkers with the line, "Got

In the green and gold, and going for it at the Gabba. When the time finally came to
fight out a Shield final there, I couldn't make it, being away on "green and gold business".
It remains one of my great disappointments.

A cast of captains. Queensland's first Sheffield Shield, guarded by former and current captains. From back row, left, to front row, right: Lew Cooper, Jeff Thomson, Tom Veivers, Ron Archer, Stuart Law, Geoff Dymock, Mike Lucas, Rob Kerr, Jack McLaughlin, Sam Trimble, me, John Maclean, Allan Border, Greg Chappell.

On the way to the green and gold; the Australian Under-19 team to England in 1983. I'm front row, left. Others who went on to play for Australia were Craig McDermott (seventh from left, back row), Tony Dodemaide (second from right, back row) and Mike Veletta (fourth from right, front row).

Hamming it up with AB.

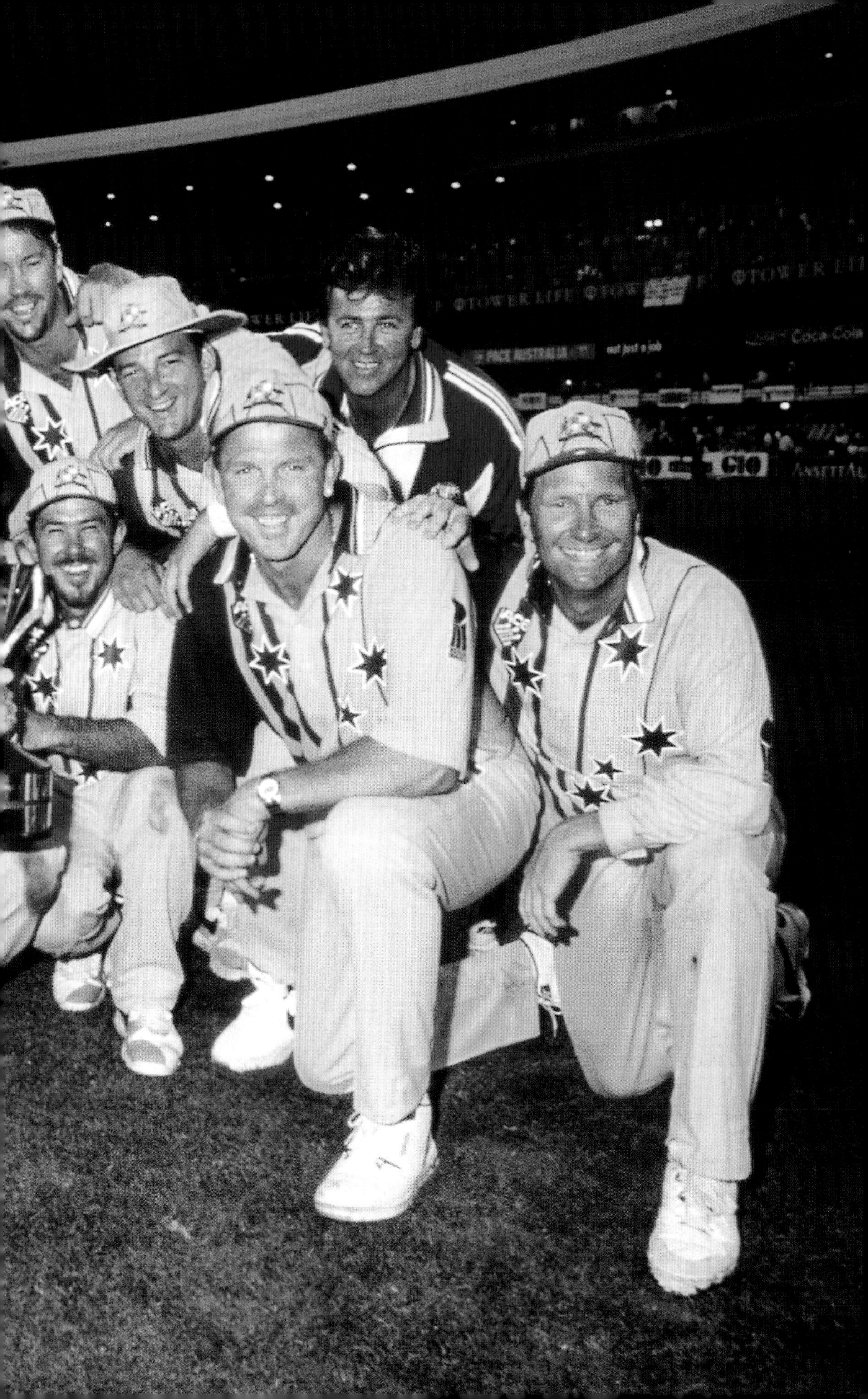
TOWER LIFE
TOWER LIFE
Coca-Cola
not just a job
GIO

VIV JENKINS/PBL MARKETING

Even as a boy soldier in Biloela I fancied a hat with the Aussie emblem, and winning the "baggy green" was a dream come true.

Previous pages: I'm all in favour of the practice of winners grinning. After a rough start to my Australian career there have been more celebrations than wakes. I try to enjoy them to the fullest, because in cricket you never know what's around the corner.

VIV JENKINS/AUSTRALIAN CRICKET BOARD

My first Aussie training camp was tough going for a new boy, but my first tour was a nightmare.

Ready for snicks at the Gabba, ready for slices at Sharjah.
Golf is the preferred relaxation for most of the Aussie team.

a bit a good news for ya ... we've won the Shield" and they, feigning excitement, would say, "That's terrific, good on you ... er, what Shield was that?"

I was genuinely upset at missing our moment of glory. "It's a disaster, an absolute disaster. The most disappointing moment of my career," I told anyone who asked. A bit over the top? Not at all, I would have loved to have been there. I had even harboured the hope that the team might ring me every other minute during the match with the news, "We're going well." My wife Helen was ringing me with constant updates; she was genuinely excited and because Helen rarely got that way over a cricket game, I thought, "If Helen's excited what must the rest of the State be like?"

And I had these visions of groups of ex-Queensland players watching the game, sipping a cold beer, willing the team on, and, at the end of each day dissecting the state of play then going home, very late. But could there ever have been a better excuse for being late for dinner? I dearly wanted to be part of it and, quite frankly, I felt envious that I wasn't.

So why did Queensland take so long to win the Shield? From my earliest years in the Queensland side I developed a theory that the Maroons suffered badly from a lack of cohesion. Former Queensland captain Bill Brown has told me that in the early days the Maroons had limited playing strength and that generated humble expectations. I am sure a little bit of this thinking was passed on down the generations. In ensuing years it's been my view that a two-tiered class system comprising internationals and the Shield players had a ruinous effect on the team.

The precious quality called team unity was undermined by the dreaded "I've played 20 Tests and you haven't" syndrome. Judgments made on our Shield cricketers were all based on cricketing achievements, and never mind the fact that the player might have a fine intellect and a highly respected job. Sadly, all such judgments did was to make the Shield player feel smaller. The result was many talented cricketers just drifted along without the encouragement and guidance that is a vital pep pill for all fringe players.

Queensland's problems trace back several generations. My former employer Bill Buckle, a one-time Queensland batsman, once told me former Test wicket-keeper Wally Grout would explode if Bill threw the ball too hard to him in a Shield match.

If this happened early in the day Bill would spend the rest of day worrying about hitting the gloves properly which could only have distracted his focus on the remainder of the game.

I believe that a lot of Queensland Sheffield Shield players never felt comfortable speaking their mind when the international players were back in the team. For instance, Greg Chappell's commanding aura seemed to intimidate a lot of squad players.

Greg remembers finishing Sheffield Shield games at the Gabba when the

My first taste of the "monkey". The Queensland State primary schools Under-12
rugby league team, 1976, lost the series 1-2 to NSW. Some of my team-mates were:
Mark Hohn (No. 17), Michael Hagan (No. 6), Danny Stains (No. 8), Steve Carter (No. 9)
and Peter Jackson (No. 14). I'm second inset, left.

boys would be heading somewhere for a steak and no-one would bother inviting him. They assumed that Greg would have too much on his plate to worry about their problems, that he was so busy he'd have other more important commitments, or he would want to see his family—so they made the decision for him. Perhaps that's why, in the early 1980s, the Queensland players voted Gary Cosier as their representative to the ACB ahead of Greg, who at the time was Australian captain. It was a barrier that had to be broken down if Queensland were to come good.

New South Wales have never had this problem and I'm sure it's one of the reasons they've been such a strong, successful side. The NSW State boys often take the micky out of the internationals, which encourages mateship and equality. Steve Waugh is renowned for keeping an eye on grade results and at mid-week training he often talks to the young players about their weekend performances. Queensland is gradually moulding an ethos similar to this and the State is the better for it.

Queensland may not win the Shield every second year but they have become a strong, independent side. When I return to State level during the season

I feel I am slotting into a tight team unit and the pressure is on me to perform well. The surging confidence of the side is reflected in the smallest mannerisms. I used to be hesitant about telling too many Australian team stories around the Queensland boys for fear of sounding a big head, but now they will match every story with one of their own. That old inferiority complex is history.

So, at St Lucia it was a real treat to at last turn the mortar gun on those painful Australian team-mates who, over seven years of Test cricket, had treated us Maroons as a joke, as if our State cap had a little helicoptor fixed to the top of it. You don't reckon I enjoyed opening fire on the Waughs and Mark Taylor the day we won it.

Carl Rackemann arrived in Barbados a few days after the Shield win, armed with "Sheffield Shield champions" t-shirts. We wore them to breakfast—11 mornings in a row! The other players made an effort to eat before or after us.

And I insisted that I share a room with Carl when he arrived, for though I had received many updates about the final I was desperate to relive the occasion through Carl's eyes and soak up every last skerrick of the five fantastic days.

I have enjoyed the company of many players in the Sheffield Shield ranks but few as much as Carl Rackemann, who has inspired several of my thoughts about loyalty in life. Carl is as loyal to his family, friends, country people and to cricket as any person could be. His middle name is Gray but he sees most things in black and white.

When Powers were sponsoring Queensland cricket he did heaps of work for them, yet when XXXX took over he was as dutiful as he had been with Powers. I can just imagine Carl making a decision to throw all his Powers gear out the day XXXX signed.

People might think that is an example of faltering loyalty but that is mistaken. Carl is fiercely loyal to Queensland cricket and if that means hopping the fence to support a sponsor he will do it because that's what is best by his State.

The deep fondness with which Carl speaks of his many friends in cricket makes you think that when your back is turned he will speak fondly of you as well.

Channel Nine's commentary team rang me at 2.30am St Lucia time, a bizarre time to be interviewed, but I had no complaints because it made me feel part of the occasion. Just to hear the sound of the crowd coming through the other end of the line gave me a buzz.

My joy at Queensland's success contrasted Steve Waugh's distress; he wrote in his diary: "Whether South Australia will be allowed to enter the competition next season is still to be confirmed."

A major catalyst behind the establishment of a more equitable policy was John Buchanan's appointment as Queensland coach. John was a fringe Queensland player in the 1970s, and is living testimony to my point about the "us versus them" mindset. I'll bet anything that John was one of those fringe players who wouldn't have felt all that confident speaking up in the presence of the big names that graced the team in those days. I know that because the day before applications closed for the Queensland coaching job John came around to my place, still hesitant about whether he should apply.

He said he would not apply if he thought he was going to have problems with any of the senior players. Shades of the past.

I went through it with him and I could see no problems. Allan Border would do whatever it took to win the Shield, so he would cooperate with whomever was coach. McDermott and I would be absent for most of the season, so that left Carl Rackemann, whose deep-seated friendship with previous coach Jeff Thomson could have been a concern. But we knew Rackemann, and we knew Rackemann's respect for the Queensland side would override any residual problems lingering after Thommo lost the coaching job. So I guaranteed Buchanan the senior players would not be a problem.

'Pluto' Buchanan coached me in the Queensland Colts side in the early 1980s and I was impressed by his meticulous research. Every Wednesday at the Gabba he would have the clippings of all the results from the weekend's grade games and run through our opponents, player by player, developing a game plan for the following weekend.

John felt there had to be a stepping stone between grade and Shield cricket and was a vocal advocate of an expanded State second XI fixture list. The idea was quashed at the time but came into vogue a decade later. Under Buchanan Queensland now incorporates second XI and Colts training with Shield squad practice, a major breakthrough, for it means players of all standing are mixing well and the days of the best and the rest are gone, hopefully forever. In some ways he was ahead of his time.

Queensland have had an interesting range of coaches. Jeff Thomson coached us for four years and as a reader of the game he was spot on. He could sniff out body language as quickly and as accurately as those infamous West Indian quicks and knew what we should be thinking when we went out, and what our opponents would be mulling over as well. Beneath the froth and bubble of Thommo's colourful sermon's lay general good sense.

But I don't feel he put as much quality time into the job as it required. He didn't utilise the services of ex-champions and could have made more use of the QCA staff, for there are now two or three coaches at training lending valuable expertise to the cause. Thommo didn't coach technically in some areas, either. He would say he was available when anyone needed him, but most of the players just didn't feel right asking him to stay back for half

*Meeting the great Carl Rackemann. He presented me with my Queensland
Under-16 cap. With Carl, closest to camera, is Greg Ritchie. Later we became
team-mates. In the background, partially obscured by Carl, is Kevin Langer,
older brother of Allan 'Alfie' Langer. Both the Langer boys represented
Queensland in junior cricket.*

an hour after training. I feel he wasn't pro-active enough in identifying a batsman's weakness and saying, "You're with me for an hour on the bowling machine from 7pm on Wednesday."

John Bell fulfilled only one year of a three-year term because he became too gung-ho too quickly. He had some good ideas and I don't think anyone could say the logic he was preaching wasn't sound, but before charging in like a modern day Napolean he should have worked on strengthening his relationships with the players. He should have found out more about what made everyone else tick before imposing himself so strongly.

Richie Robinson, the dynamic former Victorian captain and wicket-keeper did a sound job, but he was one of the most nervous people I have seen.

Melbourne Cup king Bart Cummings has often said that for a horse to be primed for the Cup it must cover a certain amount of kilometres in training over the previous few months. Richie would cover this amount in one day watching a Shield match. When we were fielding he would circle the ground, clipboard in hand, making notes and occasionally breaking into a fast trot. How he survived his one summer in charge without having a heart attack I will never know. He couldn't have been that nervous as a player because he would not have been the high class cavalier he was.

When I first entered the Sheffield Shield arena in 1987 I was stunned by the lack of planning and goal-setting in the Queensland side. Allan Border's philosophy was to try as hard as he could every ball and to expect everyone else to do the same. But he wasn't what you'd call a motivator, or a goal-setter in the strictest sense of the term.

In my view there are always ways of making a player try that little bit harder and to be that bit more aware of what could be achieved in any particular session. Consequently you feel great when you come off after that session if you've achieved your goal. If you haven't, you know you have extra work to do in the next session to make up for falling short of your plan.

But AB was not that sort of player. He would say, "If we set our goal for a session at 3/60 what happens if we get 3/10, do we just let them have 50?"

Of course you don't. You reframe your goals in five seconds flat and try just as hard in pursuit of them.

In those early days for Queensland I quite often thought, "Where are all the team talks, the planning, the getting in and supporting each other ... we are just drifting along."

I had no idea what other players were thinking or what they were planning. We were just like 11 little individual units all doing our own thing. Even in club cricket at Norths our planning seemed a professional level above what was going on in the Queensland side. I still believe cricketers are years behind other sports in the concept of goal-setting.

I was really disappointed in what was going on and the segregated na-

On the catwalk in 1995, modelling the Bulls' new range of leisure wear.

ture of the team did not impress me. It was at this time that I first developed a firm relationship with Test allrounder and current chairman of the Australian Test selection panel Trevor Hohns.

I felt comfortable pouring out my frustrations to Trevor; I would say, "Shouldn't this be happening, shouldn't we be setting goals and targets rather than going out as 11 individuals?"

'Cracker' would say, "Yeah, I know what you are saying but it is just something that happens ... we go on this way all the time."

When Hohns later became captain he proved an excellent skipper, a thoughtful and at times firm man-manager who tended to get the best out of players. He led through example and effort but would pull guys into line with a disciplined hand if they needed it.

Another controversial feature of Queensland cricket was the imported international players, the stars—were they good for us, or did they undermine the cause?

The Queensland dressing room has hosted two high class English imports in my time—Ian Botham and Graeme Hick—and I enjoyed the company of both. Hick is a fine bloke whom I rated highly as a player. But it seemed he was never at peace with the burden of high expectation that was a stone in his shoe every step he took in Test cricket.

In a sport whose combatants come in a multitude of shapes and sizes, Hick stands out as the perfect physical specimen. Few players hit the ball as hard as Hick, and to see him bludgeon a cricket ball gives you the impression that he is one of the game's truly hard men who would exude strength and a commanding bearing off the field as well.

But he is not a hard man at all, and is actually quite shy, sensitive and quietly spoken. He hails from a tobacco farm in Harare, loves the quiet life at Worcester and admitted the scorching spotlight of international cricket genuinely intimidated him in the first few years.

He once confessed to being fascinated at the irony of being one of the most pumped up, shot down, criticised and analysed players of his era when, in his own words, "I am a very plain, straightforward person."

His technique had its foibles, particularly against the short ball, where he used to become tucked up by taking his back foot towards square leg rather than back and across towards the off side as the text book tells us we should.

Moving to leg left Graeme vulnerable on two fronts—most obviously to the nick to slips which is a consequence of not getting behind the ball and also, the one that followed him towards leg, the hastened, awkward tuck to a close-in catcher.

Test cricket's worst kept secret and most obvious game plan was fashioned around Graeme's reluctance to get behind the line of the ball. He was bombarded with countless waist-to-shoulder balls and it is to his credit that he fought his way through the numbing trough that caused him so much anguish at the start of his career. It ultimately hardened him for the long road ahead.

Graeme had to inject a few steel pellets in his mellow nature to adjust to the gamesmanship which can be a disconcerting part of Test cricket. I've read that he once saw a psychologist who took him through a series of seven stages dealing with the mental side of Test cricket, and the last one was coping with verbal abuse.

Once in England in 1993, when he flayed a four off Shane Warne, one of our fieldsman said to him, "That's all right big fella. You have a hit because guess who's coming on with the new ball. It's big Merv and we know where he's going to bowl don't we."

Apart from the occasional technical flaw there has to be a reason why Hick's rich talent has not produced a landslide of runs at Test level. One of my theories is that verbals such as this would distract him and make him lose concentration.

Botham was simply an indomitable showman. No cause was ever lost to him. I had only played a couple of first-class matches when I started to follow the great I T Botham in the Queensland batting order. Nobody is perfect and Both had his critics for his infamous misbehaviour on a flight to Perth and for not attending net training, which he hated on the basis that he disliked hitting a ball in a confined space.

It has been said that he caught more barramundi than balls at training during his time in Queensland and it is true that he missed at least half the practice sesssions.

At the time it meant nothing to me for I was simply happy to focus on my own game, but if it happened today I would be most critical of him.

The 1987 season, before Queensland were known as The Bulls, but Ian Botham went on the rampage anyway. I'm still not quite sure why we didn't win the Shield that year. The man at first slip is Dav Whatmore, today Sri Lanka's coach, then a batsman for Victoria.

The whole ethos of a successful side involves everyone rowing in the same direction.

You can't have 10 players pulling their weight while the 11th is pulling up a crab pot somewhere in Moreton Bay. He should have been setting the example and been the first at training. How we managed not to win the Shield in Botham's year is beyond me. Can you believe that we won four out of our first five games to be on 24 points halfway through the summer?

For all that I believe England's decision to overlook him as a selector is a poor one, because he is a fine judge of temperament and recognises the qualities a player needs to be successful.

I believe the continued presence of the imported players tempted Queensland players to sit back, expecting the import to steer the side. I also believe the players began to expect this of the Australian players in the side when they were off Test duty. But as cricket's international program has become more and more saturated, the internationals return to the interstate scene tired, sometimes on a bit of a downer, and just want to be treated like any other player.

That's why it made sense for Allan Border not to be captain of Queensland while he was captain of Australia. The best way for Queensland to get the most from Border was to let him relax and simply be a player, letting his understudy keep the reins, absorbing advice from him.

I'm sure it also helped to break down the class system, an event that was one of the great unrecognised forces behind Queensland winning the Shield.

One crucial element of success in Sheffield Shield cricket is to hold onto high class players who are over 30 years—those who have either faded from the Test scene or will never make it.

I am an unabashed admirer of the way New South Wales play their cricket. Steve Small never played a Test match and was a most unorthodox player, yet even in his late 30s he was a wonderfully competitive role model for young NSW players. Queensland are gradually acquiring some of the strengths of NSW cricketers—they are confident, quite self-centred and highly opinionated—but it worries me that a lot of the 30-plus players at club level in Queensland—the Steve Smalls—are leaving the game.

Cricket must provide incentive for players of the 30–35 age bracket to stay in the game, not scare them off. My brother Ken told me that his Brisbane club side Wynnum-Manly conducted an exhaustive pre-season fitness campaign which involved a series of 400 metre sprints on Sunday morning just to prepare for one game a week.

You don't need to be that fit to play club cricket. We need to be careful we don't weed out "the old heads" of the game just because they can't quite match it with the "young legs".

DARK DAYS
OF CHARACTER

"It is no good crying over spilt milk.
All you can do is bail up another cow."

J B CHIFLEY

"In September 1988 Ian Healy was a humble young man with plenty to be humble about." So wrote *The Australian's* Terry Brindle on the verge of my first Australian tour, which was to become a nightmare start to my international career.

The team to tour Pakistan had been chosen in March, but did not leave until September. I prepared exhaustively, even commissioning my father-in-law Don Perkins to take me to Brisbane's top curry houses, where several itchy scalps and sweaty foreheads later I felt as ready as I ever would be for the culinary challenge ahead. I wondered if I had jumped on the wrong plane when the first meal I had in Lahore was eggs on toast for breakfast.

On the cricket side my first outings as Australia's 'keeper-elect were in the novel setting of the Brisbane Warehouse competition's winter league where I played for Mater Hill; I became instantly aware of the increased pressure that accompanied my elevated standing in the game. Up until then, to my mates I had been the rookie of whom not a lot was expected. Suddenly I was Australia's new Test gloveman and was expected to perform without blemish.

But mostly on my mind was Greg Chappell's pre-tour talk in which he had rammed home several important points such as (a) look beyond Pakistan and make a long-term plan; (b) you won't find anything harder than Pakistan; and (c) within Pakistan there will be no greater challenge than Karachi.

Greg's words were to become starkly prophetic.

We had suspected that the Pakistanis would try to nail us on a crumbling pitch in the First Test then produce two tracks as flat as the Nullarbor Plain. And indeed the Karachi pitch was a treacherous looking piece of ground, a shifting jigsaw which looked three days old on the first morning.

The pitch was so dry it could have been declared drought-stricken, while the lush surrounds could have been transplanted from Huntingdale Golf Club.

Allan Border, then a Test cricket journeyman of a decade's experience, later described the wicket as "the worst I have ever seen—you name it, it's got it".

Within the first hour of the First Test the ball was fizzing around like a mad bumble bee and turning shoulder high. We had our spinners—Tim May and Peter Taylor—on within 10 overs.

My confidence rose early when I pouched a fine snare off Rameez Raja from Bruce Reid's bowling, but later events that day sent me spiralling into an abyss of grieving numbness.

Javed Miandad was on 128 when he attempted a slashed cut shot off Steve Waugh. The ball fizzed through sharply and came to me at shoulder height, quite quickly because I was standing slightly shallow to off-set the low bounce.

It was no sitter but it is the type of catch that Test 'keepers should make look routine. To my absolute disgust, I dropped it. It hit my gloves and bounced out and Javed went on to make 210 as the Pakistanis batted for two days then 37 minutes on the third morning.

To compound our frustration, we were certain we had Javed twice lbw early but both appeals were turned down.

I had never played against a player who had scored 200, nor had I ever spent anything more than one day and one session in the field ... just less than half the Pakistan innings!

The longer the innings went on the more I blamed myself ... it was all my fault.

My immediate thought after dropping Miandad was, "The boys are going to hate me ... a lot of them barely know me and they will be thinking 'Who is this bloke?'"

I must have been a mental mess, because soon after dropping Miandad I apparently also missed Salim Malik.

At least that's what the records say. I was so distressed over the Miandad miss it was the only muffed chance I could remember. Even today I have no recollection of dropping Malik.

And to make the Malik spill worse, it cost Bruce Reid what would have been his first five-wicket haul in Tests, a milestone that had eluded him for the first three years of his Test career.

I have heard it said that Bruce never castigated someone for dropping a catch off his bowling, but I would have had no problems that day had he vented his spleen in my direction. In fact I would have said, "Thanks mate, I feel better now," because I was starting to become intimidated by the stony silence that was surrounding me in the dressing room.

The body language of my team-mates drove me further into my cocoon

Javed Miandad was one of world cricket's most talented batsmen, but when he seemed to be getting more benefit of the doubt from the umpires than we felt he was entitled to on my first tour to Pakistan in 1988, the team threatened to go home. All in all it was one of my blacker times in the game.

of self-doubt. David Boon, for instance, at short leg, had a habit of peering at me from under the shade of his green helmet. Never was there a hint of a smile or an encouraging "hang in there" wink and it unsettled me.

I can remember thinking, "There's another one who hates me."

Yet it was a moment in my career that probably did me a lot of good. Later I would learn this was just Boonie's natural way, that he is the type of player who doesn't put a lot of energy into others, that you have to earn your stripes before you knock around with him.

To play international cricket you need a strong hide and when a squad full of strong players and egos get together they deliberately test and toughen each other.

For instance, occasionally when batting in the nets in Pakistan someone would say to me, "Any danger of you hitting one in the middle?"

That is standard net talk, but because my self-esteem was a bit fragile it was another little piercing arrow. The moral is: It's no good looking for sympathy, it may never arrive.

Demoralised at seeing Pakistan and Miandad slip off the hook and generally depressed over our lack of success with some lbw appeals against Miandad, and poor fielding, our batting efforts disintegrated and we made just 165 (in 122 overs) and 116 (I made 26 and 21) to lose by an innings and 188 runs.

Our frustration with the umpires had been simmering since the first session of the Test when Miandad was given the benefit of several painfully close calls but the collective disdain of the side towards umpiring reached boiling point when Steve Waugh was given out lbw to left-arm spinner Iqbal Qasim, to leave us 5–54 in the first innings.

Manager Col Egar and coach Bob Simpson went to the Pakistan Board officials room to lodge a protest and later, during the tea interval, they called a group of Australian journalists to a press conference at which they criticised the pitch and umpire Mahboob Shah's decisions.

Because of my paranoid state, I tended to blame myself for the umpiring furore. My thoughts were, "If I had held those catches this would not have been a problem."

Our sense of persecution was fed by statistics about the comparison of lbw decisions received by the Pakistanis and Australians in Pakistan, which handsomely favoured the home team.

Over the next few days, the umpire issue became a matter of punch and counter punch. Simmo said, "The Pakistanis were turning around and laughing at our blokes when they were given not out after lbw appeals." Allan Border told the press, "It would seem like sour grapes after losing the Test but ultimately someone has to make a stand. I cannot believe we could bowl 170 overs and not get an lbw decision on this wicket." Pakistan batsman

*The Pakistan tour was just a warm-up for a series in Australia against
the West Indies. I filled the role of nightwatchman in the First Test at the Gabba—
and played the sweep shot to a spinner, a sight as rare in those days as a cover
drive off Malcolm Marshall, Courtney Walsh or Patrick Patterson.*

Zaheer Abbas, then the umpires boss, defended his man: "Mahboob is my best umpire. Don't blame him if the Australians misfield and drop catches."

We had a team meeting to vote on whether we should go home and when a show of hands was called for on a motion to end the tour mine shot up as if it was being jerked by a puppeteer. And, sad to say it, mainly for selfish reasons. In my state of mental dishevelment I reasoned, "This is a good chance to get out of here. I have stuffed things up a bit but if we quit the tour now I should get another chance in Australia."

I am not proud of these frail inner thoughts. These days I would not be impressed if I saw a youngster wanting to bail out of his first tour. I am sure the current side would be strong enough to absorb these types of setbacks and play on regardless.

But, apart from my self interest, I was swayed by hearing tour manager Egar, a former umpire and Board member, support the decision to abort the tour. If, as a former Test umpire and Board member, he supported the decision to abort the tour, then I had no problems lending my support.

Withdrawn and self-possessed through guilt and a lack of form, I hardly said anything in the team meetings.

After the First Test I made the following candid observation in my tour diary of our two fragile batting efforts. "Team support nil ... Players virtually thought we couldn't do it. Obviously I believed that also."

The magnitude of the crisis became apparent when a production team from Channel Nine's *60 Minutes* arrived at our Faisalabad hotel.

Displaying the type of door-barging they normally reserve for exposés of shonky car dealers, the *60 Minutes* people stormed into our breakfast room and cornered Simmo.

The Australian Cricket Board had sent a directive that no member of the party was to talk to the press, so all Simmo said was, "You are not supposed to be in here." But the crew got up our collective noses yet again when they emerged at the ground and started interviewing the locals just down in front of our dressing room.

There were questions like "What do you think of the Australians?" and answers like "They are a pack of whingers" as we twisted in our seats.

Frustrated by my form, I said to team-mates, "I can't believe how badly I am 'keeping—I have never 'kept this badly." I meant it too but I was never sure whether they believed me or whether they thought I was just looking for excuses. Their standard reply was "Just try and relax."

My six games for Queensland prior to selection were near perfect and free of great anguish and deep scrutiny. Now I was analysing myself and everyone else was analysing me as well ... the spotlight seemed to be scorching me.

Unfortunately the Australian team on that tour lacked the support system on which new players can now lean. In fact, apart from AB there weren't really any senior players, though Simmo was doing his best to keep things together.

The players were whingeing and negative in the dressing room. The older ones simply didn't want to be there.

I can remember a tour room-mate opening our motel room curtains in the morning and saying with total disgust "Oh no." Perpetually on edge, I sprung upright in bed and asked what the problem was. "It's sunny," would come the reply from a player craving for rain and a pressure-free day.

It was such a contrast to my cherished Saturdays during the Brisbane grade summer, which I'd looked forward to with a passion. Rainy summer week-ends at home were to be cursed.

If the team ethos in Pakistan had been one of positive play and support for the new bloods I could have been sucked along by it.

But inevitably I became dragged into the negative thought syndrome.

I was so wet behind the ears in big time cricket my prime yardsticks were club-related. In a letter to a friend during that tour I said, "There is not a lot of sledging in the games ... not like Norths versus Souths back home."

A year into my international career, when doing a player profile I still rated a century by my Norths team-mate Steve Monty in a QCA grade final as the best innings by a team-mate, and when I was asked to nominate the best fieldsman in Australia, I ignored all my national team-mates to go for my old buddy Inwood, who was quite exceptional.

Towards the end of the tour the players were so keen to get home they started a countdown whereby the remaining number of days were tagnamed by the jersey number worn by famous VFL or Australian rugby league play-ers. So, if there was a week to go it would be Peter Sterling day because he wore the number seven for Parramatta, New South Wales and Australia.

I was unable to relax and I felt my anguish must have been painfully ob-vious to the outside world. Crazy thoughts drifted through my head. Just before the Third Test we played a three day game in the military city of Peshawar against the North-West Frontier Province Governor's XI.

The ground, near the Afghan border, is less than 60 kilometres from the famous Khyber Pass where you can buy anything from hashish to Exocet missiles. Craftsmen in the area are so talented you can show them a gun used by John Wayne in a western movie 40 years ago and they can knock one up for you within a couple days.

As I stood in the field 'keeping, several fighter planes from the Pakistan airforce whizzed by above and I remember thinking, "If you bomb in the outfield I can get out of 'keeping for a day."

Wicket-keeping on the subcontinent is an extreme test of your physical and mental strength. Because the matches start so early you are normally at the ground at about 8.30am and walk out into a shimmering heat haze for training. The heat hits you immediately and you have barely accepted your first ball at training when your gear becomes clingy with sweat. Drenched with sweat, you later head back to the dressing room for a shower to learn that there are no cold showers, only a warm one, so you barely feel refreshed after it.

Then there is normally only one fan in the dressing room, which has a crowd around it as if someone is giving away grand final tickets.

After the First Test I resolved to work like I never have before on my game and, with golf ball and inners, retreated to a variety of brick walls in whichever centre we were staying.

I was pleased to finish the tour strongly as we almost squared the series in the final Test in Lahore. We had Pakistan reeling on the ropes at 8–153 at stumps on the final day as Taylor and May took seven wickets between them in an attack missing the tour's dominant force, Bruce Reid, who had broken down the previous day.

A few small gestures from AB towards the end of the tour meant a lot to me. During the last Test I took a diving catch to dismiss Javed Miandad and when I came to my feet Border embraced me in a bear hug as if I had just taken the catch of the century. He seemed genuinely pleased that my form was on the improve and that gave me heart.

On the way back to the team hotel after the final Test he tapped me on the shoulder and said, "You've done alright, hang in there."

Simmo also had some kind words and I was so thrilled to at last get some positive feedback I noted in my diary, "Praise from the captain and coach ... at last."

Upon touching down at Brisbane airport, AB was asked about my performance and about how my selection had placed the Queensland selectors in a quandary over what to do with Peter Anderson.

My ears pricked when I heard him say, "Ando's loss is Australia's gain." Quite a pointed statement and I thought for a moment AB had got his words wrong.

But it was a vote of support for me at a time when I needed all the support I could get.

WILD ABOUT
THE WEST

"There is nothing the body suffers that the mind may not profit by."
GEORGE MEREDITH

Far from being daunted about playing the West Indies at home for the first time I was genuinely excited by the supreme challenge of facing the game's best in the 1988–89 summer.

It turned out to be a sobering challenge. We were flogged by nine wickets in the First Test at Brisbane, trumped in the Second by 169 runs in Perth, and given one of the great physical maulings on a green wicket of variable heights in Melbourne where the West Indies used relentless pace and aggression to blast their way to victory by 285 runs.

A short anecdote provides candid evidence of how Australian teams of that era were half-beaten against the West Indies before they started.

Tim May was waiting in the Gabba dressing room to bat in the First Test with the second new ball due when several team-mates decided it was time for a bit of piss-taking. They took a new ball out of the box and whizzed it past Tim's helmet grill as he sat padded up, and then dug it into his well-nourished rib section. They asked, "How does that feel Maysie?" while he was jumping around in nervous anguish.

We all know cricketers can take themselves too seriously at times and I have great regard for the players who are the tension-breakers of the dressing room, those who can lift crestfallen team-mates from the darkest moods. But jokes like that one couldn't possibly have helped our cause. I would have much rather waited until we were in a healthy position before the shenanigans start. It is a fine line because sometimes being a bit flippant allows you to play naturally and get away with it. But in that era we weren't as tough as we should have been.

It was a much harder Australian side that arm-wrestled with the Windies four years later when, quite appropriately, May made 42 not out at Adelaide where we lost the Test by a solitary run.

The Second Test was in Perth and Geoff Marsh had warned me there wouldn't be any locals putting flowers around my neck at the airport—Perth was the home of my greatest rival, Tim Zoehrer.

He was right. There was no indication of any resentment from the locals in the street or in restaurants, just the occasional instance of people coming up to me and saying, "Sorry, but I'm a Tim Zoehrer fan and I think he should be in the side."

Fair enough. That's their opinion and good on them for sticking by their man. They never bother me. But the negative crowd reaction in the Second Test certainly did.

I never mind getting booed at the WACA in a Sheffield Shield game, for you expect it at any rival Shield venue. But a Test match is different. When Australian rugby league captain Wally Lewis was howled and baited at the Sydney Cricket Ground in the early 1980s I was thoroughly disgusted. Surely when you are playing for your country you deserve support on home soil.

There were probably no more than 20 loud-mouthed Healy-haters at the WACA but they got to me. They were sitting on the sun-drenched western terraces and they got under my skin so skilfully that I spent the day trying to impress a handful of loud-mouths rather than concentrate on the job at hand.

There was an incident when the ball was returned from the boundary and it bounced up off an awkward length and hit my thumb, dollyed in the air and I caught it before it hit the ground. It had no ramifications yet the boys in the outer were into me for 10 minutes with their "Bring back Zoehrer" chants just because I fumbled a difficult return. And they got to me.

It was only my second Test in Australia and I didn't have the mental strength to drag my thought processes back to where they should have been.

The badly cracked wicket was producing variable bounce and I had to stand closer than I would have liked as a counter measure. But, in the second innings I let through 14 byes as balls leapt off the cracks. Some flew over my head while others sprayed wildly down the leg side.

I barely left my room at night during that Test and there was a tangible sense of impending doom when Tim May, Tony Dodemaide and myself walked across the spacious park next to the WACA on the fourth evening on the way to the team motel. 'Dodders' had been belted around, Maysie dropped Viv Richards early and I was not happy with my own form. We were all really disappointed and, as you tend to be in these situations, quite fatalistic about our prospects. We fully expected it could be the last Test for all of us so we collectively decided to make hay even though the sun wasn't shining.

The next day when I went out to bat the wicket was like a jigsaw puzzle. I later wrote in my diary "Fear for life" and I meant it.

With Malcolm Marshall, Patrick Patterson, Courtney Walsh and a fairly

BRUCE POSTLE/JOHN FAIRFAX

My main adversary for the wicket-keeping spot was Tim 'Ziggy' Zoehrer,
from Western Australia, seen here celebrating an Australian Test win over England
at the SCG in 1987. With the Second Test against the West Indies in 1988 scheduled
for his home-town WACA ground, I was assured of a hot welcome,
and Ziggy's fans didn't disappoint.

useful fourth-stringer in Curtly Ambrose bearing down on a wicket doing silly things, you could die if you did something wrong. My sole thought was, "If I don't watch the ball I could get killed." So you can imagine how encouraging it was to top-score with 52. The success was to exemplify a pattern in my career where, if the gloves don't work, the bat generally does, and vice versa, but it is hell's own job to get both firing at once.

Tim 'Ziggy' Zoehrer, my closest rival for my first five years in the job, was a player I could never really work out.

I had tremendous respect for his glovemanship standing back to the fast men, particularly in Perth. I was told his work over the stumps in the eastern States wasn't quite so blemish-free, but I didn't see enough of it myself to judge.

Ziggy and I never had any personal problems with each other but, as you might expect, there was an unspoken private competition between us. We weren't the best of buddies but you certainly wouldn't call us enemies.

Tim struck me as not reading the "situation" very well. By "situation" I mean he didn't appear to have a thorough appreciation of the requirements that the forces governing Australian cricket were looking for.

He knew he was playing in the Bob Simpson era and he knew the cricketers Simpson was looking for were the hard-working types who leave no stone unturned in their preparation and put a lot of effort in with their teammates. Yet, by my yardstick, he still refused to practise very hard. On my first Ashes tour in 1989 he didn't seem to have the gloves on at training for any more than five minutes at a time in a practice session.

I couldn't work that out, for he was totally misreading the atmosphere of the team. He either bowled leg-spinners—and at that stage no-one knew he was as good as he would later prove to be—or take high balls with other fielders, but without the gloves on.

I would hit him 'keeping catches and after about 15 he would have had enough, so I would get him to hit me some and after 30 or 40 I could see he was getting bored and had had enough. So I would say, "Thanks Ziggy, have a rest," and then get someone else to hit me some more.

On the 1989 Ashes tour he had the perfect chance to take my job. I did a knee ligament in an early one-day international and missed one limited-overs international and the next county match. At that stage Ziggy was also hampered by a knee injury. During one of the matches when we were both sidelined, my brother Ken was having a beer and at the next table Ziggy was talking to some friends who asked him why he wasn't playing. He said, "Stuffed if I know, there's nothing wrong with me."

That to me summed up Ziggy—a great bloke but every now and then some things just don't quite add up. We all have our foibles—I won't pose as a plaster saint here—but that was Ziggy's chance and he missed it.

If I could take a hate-meter with me to Perth I feel it would register reduced levels each season, but the needle would have surged into the red zone with one unsavoury incident in 1992 against the West Indies.

I had made three ducks in a row, including a pair in Adelaide, so when I walked out to bat in the second innings the reception was something less than if I was the prodigal son returning.

I played and missed several times, but managed to scratch out 27 before falling to my usual push to gully. We were bowled out for 119 with Ambrose taking 7–25, including a barely believable spell of 7–1, on a miserable day.

My anguish intensified when I was followed into the players tunnel by an irate fan who threw a big ball of wet newspaper at me and said, "You are nothing but a piece of trash." It hit me in the head and shoulder and knocked my bat and gloves out of my hands.

Furious, I picked up my bat and stormed into the dressing room where there was an outcry over the incident. Security cameras traced the culprit and escorted him towards the dressing room.

I was asked if I wanted to see him, but I said no and remain forever grateful that I did, because I was so furious I was barely in control of my emotions.

Incidents like this, particularly in your home country, can be unsettling. Players can be pinched for the smallest offence, but sometimes the media are not perceptive to the type of abuse we cop.

Former chairman of Australian selectors Laurie Sawle once said that the most soul-destroying moment of his lengthy reign was our capitulation to the West Indies by 285 runs at the MCG.

It was a brutal game on a grassy, two-paced and occasionally prancing wicket which left us physically decimated. But it was also the turning point for us. We had thudded to the bottom of what seemed a bottomless barrel. But there was a firm resolve emerging by way of inward anger over our predicament that would drive Australia towards better days initially, and the pinnacle of world cricket six years later.

The Windies' nasty fasties physically decimated us at the MCG.

In the second innings I made just eight and my eyes almost water at the memory of it. In the space of 10 balls I was struck three sickening blows in the groin—twice from Ambrose and once from Walsh.

It was a strange experience because in the heat of battle I never really felt the pain. I was batting with Allan Border at the time and said to him, "Have a look at this" as I showed him my groin, which was swollen abnormally.

But the instant I returned from the crease I was overwhelmed by excruciating pain and almost fainted. My left groin was black and the rest of my private parts were covered in tiny black bruises generated when my protector, which contained small ventilation holes, was crunched into my body.

Our entire team was methodically tenderised. Graeme Wood was belted on the arm, Dean Jones was taken to hospital with rib injuries and I can recall our physio Errol Alcott sitting permanently near the dressing room door with a pain-killing spray, ready to take the field at any moment.

It was an extraordinary game. So vicious and short was the bowling that Wood, a fine stroke-maker, batted for more than a session for 12—all singles. And, after the fourth day's play fast bowler Patrick Patterson, who had one of the best Tests of his career, stormed into our dressing rooms and vented his fury—because he felt we had antagonised him when he had been at the batting crease that day!

It was such a one-way contest that even for the great Border, with all his experience, the Windies didn't bother having a mid-off, because they didn't think he, or anyone else, was capable of that routine scoring shot—the off-drive—on such a treacherous deck.

But the anger generated by this physical mauling triggered a fresh competitive spirit that was to drive Australia into a new competitive era. If there was a temporary mood of flippant defeatism in the First Test, the Melbourne Test had us brimming with determination.

We had simply had a gutful of being human targets.

We rebounded to take the next Test in Sydney, then drew the last match in Adelaide. We may not have won the series but we had our sights firmly set on revenge ... one day, somewhere, somehow.

PETER BARNES/COURIER MAIL

I'm smiling, but the big questions are, "Why is Patrick Patterson handing me back my bat?" and "Is Patrick smiling, too?"

The West Indies knew how to hurt—strike three, and I'm almost out ... on my feet! I was hit three times in the groin. The photo still makes my eyes water.

Below: *Patrick Patterson in a less expansive mood during the MCG Test in 1989, when a poor pitch made facing the West Indian pace bowlers a frightening ordeal. The batsman is Allan Border.*

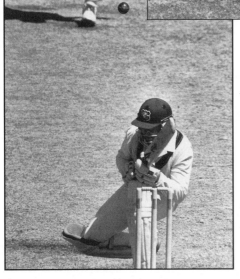

Right: *The great Curtly Ambrose. He was the "new boy" in the West Indian fast bowling quartet on the 1989 tour.*

THE DROUGHT BREAKS

"I am not good enough to be in this company but they can't kick me out now ... I am just going to bat and enjoy it."

MARK TAYLOR EARLY IN THE 1989 ASHES TOUR

Mark Taylor struggled for runs early in the 1989 Ashes tour of England, so much so that he was no certainty to open in the First Test at Headingley. After a lengthy selection meeting he got the nod and subsequently strode to a watershed summer, returning to Australia with one of the great Ashes summers of all time under his belt, 839 Test runs at an average of 83.

But Tubby's admission confirmed an old belief of mine that if an athlete has the basic honesty to admit he is struggling he has reached first base in improving his form. Tubby conceded he was trying to bat a certain number of ways to live up to people's expectations. Finally he decided he was just going to go out and have a bat and suddenly the fluffy clouds that had been clogging his thought processes were swept away.

On a tour where Australian runs flowed all summer, I managed only 103 at 17 as I battled with myself throughout the whole tour. I had only been an international cricketer for 18 months and was still learning how I should bat.

Eight years on I still don't do my best work when coming to the wicket at 4–400 like I had to in 1989, but back then I was even worse because the prowess of the top order intimidated me. I would try to bat like them, shots that simply weren't on for me.

That '89 tour started with an air of high achievement when Boonie broke Rod Marsh's beer-drinking record on the trip over. He did it the way he so often batted, with an air of quiet efficiency at the back of the plane, and with no great fuss. He only slept for nine minutes, during the descent into London, and on landing awoke and said, "That's better, I needed that kip."

No big deal was made of Boon's feat until Merv Hughes, working for an FM station in Melbourne, wound up a report with "... and the big news here is that David Boon has cracked the first 50 of the tour ...", and that led to a drama.

Merv was summoned to a special meeting with the manager Laurie Sawle and Simmo, who said, "Any more of this and you will be sent home." Boon was also under intense management pressure.

It seemed no-one gave us a chance on that tour, and history was running heavily against us—no Australian side had regained the Ashes in England since 1934. Our bowlers were stung by a story written by Tony Greig under a headline which suggested Australian bowlers were pussy cats. The text of the story wasn't too bad but the headline, for which Greig later apologised, made our bowling staff bristle.

It has been said so often, and it is true, that the 1989 tour saw Allan Border at his ruthless, professional best.

On the previous tour of England in 1985, Border had a great personal tour but the team failed badly. As well, he had taken some stick for mixing socially with Ian Botham and David Gower. Ian Chappell had lectured him: "AB, I don't mind you getting beaten by the West Indies or Pakistan but I can't stand it when you get beaten by the Poms. While you are being nice to them they are caning your backside."

It roused in AB the all-consuming goal of winning the Ashes.

AB only broke his self-imposed social ban near the end of the tour when the Ashes had been reclaimed. Then he went to Gower's place in Leicestershire.

Merv, looking every inch the English gentleman, right up to his raised eyebrows, discreetly hidden beneath the bowler hat.

COURIER-MAIL

He said to Gower, "David, the last time we came here I was a nice guy who finished last. I've been through all sorts of ups and downs with my team, but this time I thought we had a bloody good chance and I was prepared to be as ruthless as it takes to stuff you. I didn't mind upsetting anyone, my own team-mates included, so long as we got the right result."

My form throughout the tour was not great. I was shackled by anxiety. I felt like I was in the midst of grand performers and I was just plodding.

It was not until I returned in 1993 that I realised just how intense I had been four years before. On the second visit I noticed and enjoyed many aspects of England that had been nothing more than a featureless blur for me in '89. In 1993 I made time to smell the flowers, as they say.

My tour diary from '89 brims with statements of self-admonishment such as, "Not running enough ... lift your game ... too many thoughts and worries, not single-minded enough ... withdraw from the atmosphere and concentrate ... thinking too much, adding pressure ... love your job."

While I missed plenty of chances with the gloves in the county games, I didn't miss one in the Tests, though I couldn't escape the barbs of the English media. One writer described me as Teflon Gloves—nothing sticks.

I felt the rating of my tour was encapsulated by a conversation with Geoff Lawson on the plane home. He was writing a tour diary and rating the performance of every player, but I had him stumped. He knew he couldn't pay me a huge compliment, but on the other hand he knew I hadn't done much wrong. In those days I always got reports like, "Safe, doesn't do a lot wrong."

After we were thumped in the first one-day international at Manchester I was involved in a comical mix-up in the second at Nottingham. I had come to the wicket with Australia needing 53 off 10 overs, but wrenched my right knee turning for a third run with Steve Waugh, who was run out after I slipped. Talk about a mess! I battled on for a few overs in pain before finally requesting a runner, Dean Jones.

Then, as the match was boiling up to a breathless finish, with seven balls to go I got one through the infield and scampered through for two—forgetting all about my runner!

The crowd roared as the three of us bolted through and, to make matters worse, I beat Deano home.

England's captain David Gower saw the funny side of it—he walked past me and muttered something about me being faster than Carl Lewis, then gave Deano a 'red card' with the words "Thanks for popping in." That—the dismissal of Jones was unnecessary—infuriated AB because he believed I could have done myself further injury.

We scrambled a tie on the last ball of the match after I galloped through for a bye to 'keeper Steve Rhodes, who missed the stumps with his under-armed throw.

We snared a last over victory in the third one-dayer at Lord's, but I was missing. The next few weeks of the tour were a pain, because the knee took some time to heal, but no moment was more painful than when physio Errol Alcott took the sticking plaster off—and layers of skin with it!

Mark Taylor, the player who felt he was struggling to tread water in international cricket, made a patient and priceless 136 in our 210-run First Test win at Headingley. Afterwards he made the point that he had now played three Tests for two wins and a draw—and could not understand why people thought Test cricket was a hard game!

Steve Waugh, who had been waiting three years for his first Test century, made 173 not out and Terry Alderman took match figures of 10–151 to win a magnum of champagne which he refused to open, not because he's selfish but because he's superstitious. Terry has always been a stickler for the "it ain't over til the fat lady sings" theory. "Put it on ice until we win the Ashes," he said.

Alderman mesmerised England. He was a tough, occasionally stubborn man with strong opinions, whose company I loved. He simply knew he was going to excel on that tour. And I admired the way he put in so much effort helping the other bowlers.

Dean Jones ruffled Terry's feathers when he said in a newspaper article soon after our return that Alderman did not actually bowl an outswinger and his success was partly due to the con job of making the English believe he swung the ball. What Deano tried to say was that the outswinger was the softener which lulled the batsmen into thinking everything was going away from the bat. The balls which really did the damage were the ones that straightened through the air or off the seam to batsmen who expected the ball to go the other way.

This was an extraordinary win. We set them 402 to win on the last day and with just one wicket down at lunch on a lifeless deck, we thought we were no chance to win but were quietly satisfied about the fact that we couldn't lose. But we surged through their middle order after the break to skittle them for 191 with 90 minutes to spare.

After the way Ian Botham humbled Australia at Headingley at 1981 you can imagine the joy that engulfed survivors from that tour, Allan Border and Geoff Lawson.

Border was hosed with beer on the team balcony during a television interview, and at the Pier 6 bar and bistro next to the team hotel, the Copthorne. In the midst of our partying that night, I unveiled a new impersonation of the Tim May delivery. It started outside the door to the beer garden, angled in and around tables occupied by goggle-eyed patrons, stretched the length of the bar and culminated in a phantom delivery outside the women's toilets.

One of the kinder media descriptions of England's Test performance was "a lily-livered, limp-wristed" surrender.

The English media is a world of total extremes. You are either a super-hero or a total dunce. They hate a "5–230 at stumps" day because there are no heroes and villains.

I have heard a story about one newspaper editor's approach to the Ashes Test in Nottingham in 1993 when Gooch waited until well into the last morning before declaring against us. It looked like a case of over-cautiousness until we lost six wickets by tea.

The sports editor rang his man at the ground to say that their paper was going with the headline "Captain Cool" which was to laud Gooch's decision. But when Brendon Julian and Steve Waugh saved the Test for Australia it became "Captain Cockup".

In some of the real drum-beating tabloids, cricket doesn't even get a run in the paper early in the season unless something controversial is happening.

Mike Gatting once said that when the English side goes bad, it generates a competition between the papers to say how bad they are going. They have made some fools out of some fine cricketers and men and that disturbs me. During that series they nicknamed the side 'Gower's Goons' and, using artificial imagery, had the team dressed in bizarre fools' hats that made them look like total buffoons.

When John McEnroe appeared at Wimbledon they superimposed his head on a naked body standing on a tennis court and ran it on the front page. You had to wait until the last paragraph of the story before you learnt it was a mock photo. This one, however, doesn't count in the list of offensive photos, because apparently McEnroe loved it.

One of the most famous tabloid gimmicks was a promotion by *The Sun* in the late 1980s, when it gave away 1500 Shakoor Rana dart boards so that fans could take out revenge on the Pakistani umpire who drove Gatting into a finger pointing rage on the subcontinent.

But say what you like about the tabloids (most people do). Call them over-the-top, reckless and unfair in their judgements of people—they are the first thing you pick up in the morning.

Breakfast chatter is often broken with a paper-reading player saying, "Listen to this ..." During the 1993 tour Ted Dexter banned the tabloid from the English dressing room because of the savage way the papers attacked his side. The ban didn't even last 24 hours before one of the players arrived with a copy of *The Sun*.

It's tradition that on the last day of the Lord's Test, the Second, the Queen greets the Australians. I remember she had a very soft handshake and a well-used smile—it didn't warm my heart, but then again it might well have been her millionth greeting of the year.

It's a big moment and the team gets a bit anxious about it. Simmo gave us a protocol briefing: "Shake her hand lightly and say 'Good afternoon Maa'm' and, if she does not want to continue the conversation, simply let her move on." I think she was less than impressed that some of the boys hadn't shaved.

As I watched her walk away I wondered if Her Majesty harboured an expectation of one day eclipsing King George V as "the last English monarch to shake the hand of a winning English captain against Australia at the home of cricket". Of the 21 Ashes Tests played at Lord's since the turn of the century England has won only one.

We certainly didn't help her out, winning by six wickets in a match which featured Terry Alderman taking his almost mandatory nine wicket haul, Steve Waugh 152 not out and David Boon (94), with his parents in the grandstand, just missing what would have been his first Test century in England. He would curse himself for another four years.

This was a breakthrough tour for Steve Waugh. My everlasting memory of him was his brimming confidence. I can still see him padded up in the dressing room saying, "You know I feel great again today." He scored 506 runs at 126.5 on that 1989 tour.

A six wicket victory might seem like a walk in the park but the last day, with so much at stake, was full of tension. It took us almost an hour to get the last English wicket. The storm clouds looming ominously when we left the field broke open during the lunch break and we lost an hour's play.

Then we subsided to 4–67 when Allan Border hit one down the throat of fine leg; he came off, worried, and sought solace in the shower, unable to bear watching as Tugga Waugh and Boonie advanced our score slowly towards victory. And there he stayed, ordered by the rest of us not to move. Another cricketing superstition: don't move when things start to go well.

Poor old AB looked like he had just swum the English channel when we allowed him back into the room to watch Tugga crack a back foot cover drive through the off-side for victory.

We took a 2–0 lead. Deep emotions were starting to well within the touring party but the celebration was quite restrained as we kept an eye on the big picture ... we still hadn't won the Ashes.

At this point of the series we could sense English morale was starting to sag. Mike Gatting, who played just one Test, was not the batsman he was a couple of years earlier and his body language was that of a man bereft of confidence.

The droop-shouldered way in which he walked to the wicket gave off an aura of vulnerability; you just got the feeling that something bad was going to happen to him and it normally did.

I might have felt more sympathy for him if I hadn't been an Australian fighting for The Ashes—and if he hadn't referred to me as 'Tim' throughout my entire career, as in Tim Zoehrer.

I had been watching or listening to Ashes battles since I was in short pants in Biloela yet not until I sampled the rich emotion of our dressing room at Old Trafford in 1989 did I appreciate the whole passionate ethos of Ashes cricket.

AB is not what you would call an emotional bloke yet, in his unrehearsed speech to the players in the dressing room the day we won back The Ashes he was as moved as I have ever seen him.

"This means a lot to me ... and I want to thank you ... you blokes deserve all the accolades you get ... you have done really well ..." and at this point he drifted out of the speech and his lips started to quiver.

Henry Lawson shed tears and for once cast aside his teetotaller habits and swigged a bottle of champagne in the corner with Alderman. The two veterans of so much Ashes heartache back in 1981 looked at each other and agreed, "We will never be back here ... let's enjoy it."

As victory loomed I had thought it was just a slightly special series win. Yet to see the unrestrained joy on the faces of four old-timers—Border, Alderman, Lawson and Trevor Hohns—told me Ashes cricket was on a plane all of its own. It would be a shame if that passion was ever lost; as a senior player I have to foster the feeling in the side that the lustre surrounding the Ashes should remain special forever.

We only needed 81 runs in our second innings to win The Ashes and got them one wicket down. It triggered what was described as the most memorable balcony scene since Romeo and Juliet.

We took the bus to Nottingham for a three-day game starting the next day and even that routine trip provided an unforgettable moment.

A group of promotional girls were travelling along the motorway in a minibus beside us and we urged our driver to go at the same speed so we could trade banter.

In our tiddly state we traded waves and victory signs then, without any urging from us, the girls stood up in their bus, dropped their pants and pressed their naked bottoms to the window. And we thought winning the Ashes was big!

The night had a comical twist to it when Steve Waugh and I did a radio interview to Melbourne masquerading as each other.

Steve took the phone first and said he was Ian Healy and told the announcer things like, "Sooner or later in this series I hope to score a run and take a catch," then I grabbed the phone and said I was Steve Waugh, adding, "I'm working on my bowling, but it is hard because you know what I am like, always injured."

Totally smashed we giggled our way through it, never giving a thought

Martin Crowe looks just a little guilty, I'm sure he's out. My exuberant appealing has got me into trouble occasionally, but there was a time in my career when I was accused of not appealing enough!

Ouch! I'm led off the MCG by the Aussie physiotherapist Errol Alcott after taking one near the eye. David Gower had padded up to a ball from Greg Matthews and it had ricocheted up into my face, an ever-present danger for any 'keeper standing up to spinners. But the good times far outweigh the bad—stumping off-spinners are a great source of satisfaction. In trouble are New Zealand's Test opener Blair Pocock (opposite page top) and Sri Lanka's Asanka Gurusinghe (opposite page bottom).

Tough, eh? A magic moment atop Table Top mountain with Steve Waugh and Matt Hayden on the 1994 tour to South Africa.

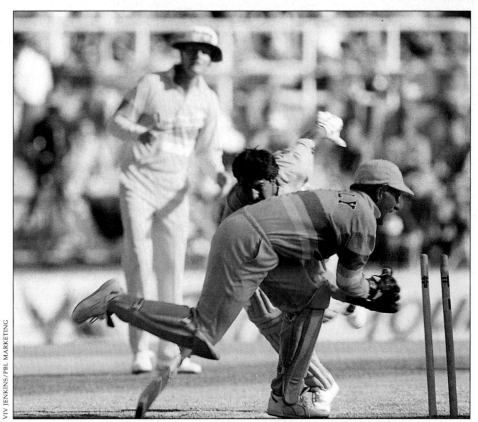

I soon found out you need a thick skin to be part of the Aussie cricket team. On the field your team-mates might be hearty back-slappers after a dismissal, but off the field they'll be planning the best way to "take the mickey". One such ruse is the "Daktari"—awarded to any player who, according to his fickle team-mates, commits a daft act. Matt Hayden was just one victim on the 1993 Ashes tour (opposite page).

In the middle of a run chase in a day-nighter at Cape Town.

Feeling good. Australia on the balcony at The Oval after the last Test in the series.

GRAHAM MORRIS/LONDON

GRAHAM MORRIS/LONDON

Reminiscing after a great tour. We get to sample some of the sponsor's product.
From the left, Geoff Marsh, me, Bob Simpson, Merv Hughes,
Greg Campbell and Trevor Hohns bask in Ashes glory after the final Test.

to the wide audience who would be listening back home and probably conclude we were hopeless, self-critical jibberers. Later I ran into Test selector Jim Higgs, who said he'd heard the interview in Melbourne and picked both our voices.

Always one to enjoy a practical joke, Higgsy said he had a bit of a laugh as I wondered whether anyone else had realised what was going on.

We won the Fifth Test at Trent Bridge by an innings and 180 runs. Swampy Marsh and Tubby Taylor, who batted through the first day to leave us 0–301 at stumps, were tired at the end of the day although David Boon, the batsman who sat padded up all day, claimed to be more mentally wrung out than both of them!

I made one and five, so my poor batting form continued. Worse still, I sustained a facial cut which required four stitches after being struck by one from Cracker Hohns that turned out of the footmarks. Worst of all I had to

COURIER-MAIL

Street parades were all the rage when the victorious 1989 team came home.
This is how Brisbane welcomed the four Queenslanders.

Opposite page: *In 1991, after retaining The Ashes we won in 1989.*
Bruce Reid, on my left, was the bowling hero.

GREGG PORTEOUS/NEWS LTD

go to hospital to be stitched while the boys celebrated, this being the occasion when big Merv sustained a marathon effort to drink the entire cocktail list at the team hotel.

Another highly unusual event took place before that Test. Graham Gooch asked to miss the Test and be sent back to county cricket to find form.

It shocked me and made me contemplate one simple question ... How bad are they travelling? No-one in the entire Australian team would even contemplate asking a selector for a favour, never mind getting permission to stand down from a Test match. I could not believe that (a) he asked the question and (b) they let him do it. I thought it was a joke.

Also, Neil Foster pulled out of one Test with a burst blister on his middle finger.

All of our bowlers have a blister on their middle finger, yet you barely hear a word of it. I could not believe the softness of English county cricket.

GAMESMANSHIP

"Beat your rival in the mind, everything else will fall into place."
OLD PROVERB

I think one of the great fascinations in cricket is trying to work out what your rival is thinking.

What's in his mind that made him do that? That's how I think. Sometimes I confuse people but I really enjoy trying to go the extra step deeper.

A key to exerting pressure is understanding body language. The more you play against different people the more you understand their body language, and the 'keeper should be able to pick up signals better than anyone.

In trying to pick chinks in the armour of any quarry you look for inconsistencies. When I looked up at the television during the Trinidad Test of our last West Indian tour and saw Curtly Ambrose doing a media interview, I felt it was a great breakthrough for the Australian side.

Why? Because when he is going well he spurns them. In his first six years of international cricket he barely did an interview yet the pressure of moderate performance in the West Indies obviously led him to adopt a more mellow approach.

South African fast bowler Allan Donald has very revealing body language which makes his thoughts an open book for all to see. He is a bowler you can get on top of at times. You see him castigating himself for bad deliveries and you think you can take him down and out of the attack.

Whereas his team-mate Fanie de Villiers never drops his guard and always gives the impression he is indomitable.

Good conditions or bad, on his day, or yours, he just keeps plugging away with the same body language whether he is getting flogged or not.

You never know too much about how he is thinking and I admire him for that. I have seen him say to batsmen at the end of play "Gee you really pasted me during that period — I didn't have any idea where to bowl to you."

But a few hours earlier you would not have known he was thinking that for his inner thoughts were so well disguised.

One of the reasons why the West Indians rate David Boon so highly is that his body language never changes. If you slotted in a video of Boon batting during the peak of his great years in the early 1990s and then substituted it with a video of him out of form you wouldn't notice one discernible change in his body language. His only slight giveaway is that when he is going well he has a little routine of tapping the bat behind him, raising it and dusting off the end of it, then tugging at a sleeve and adjusting his thigh pad.

I watch for the little things, a batsman banging the crease a bit harder, fidgeting a bit more, marking centre differently or accidentally dropping his bat—any change that might be a signal to the fielding side that their target is not at peace with himself.

I pick up a rhythm with batsmen. If he is just a casual bat-banger and one day he comes out when there's a bit of pressure on and bangs the bat a bit harder, his rhythm is out. This is an important time for our bowling and fielding to be good and for fieldsmen like myself to create doubts in his mind because in a few more overs he might be settled. I might say to Tubsy at slip, "Are you sure you want that gap at midwicket?—he is pretty strong there," and I know the batsman will hear it.

If he is not totally settled he will simply think, "Batsman—midwicket" and hit the ball there even though he is facing Shane Warne who spins the ball sharply away from this target area.

Some batsmen like a chat to settle their nerves, which is why it is imperative we don't always talk to them. Ian Botham was one of these. If you talked to him in an aggressive way it fired him up, if it was in a social way it calmed him down. So we said nothing.

If 'Both' was playing a nation like India or Sri Lanka his body language was swaggeringly confident to the point of being arrogant. Yet whenever he played the West Indies—against whom he had a moderate record—he became much more social because he wasn't quite at peace with himself.

Kepler Wessels was a player I made a point of chatting to, because he was an introverted character who hated chatting at the crease. If you could make him talk in any fashion, be it socially or aggressively, you had a win because he would not be the same Kepler he liked to perform as.

Steve Waugh and Brian Lara are two batsmen you never talk to at the crease and that is why it was such a poor tactical move by Curtly Ambrose to verbal Steve in the Trinidad Test in 1995.

Steve loves an old-fashioned stoush. He gets off on it. It fires up his powers of concentration. When Lara plays his natural free-flowing game he will normally give you a chance or two. If you bait Lara you risk firing him up and making him play more grimly.

The South Africans are quite adept at the verbal side of cricket and that is one of the reasons why our games with them are so evenly fought. Allan Border always used to give South Africa's Jonty Rhodes a hard time—so much so that Jonty often says, "Goodness, he was a cranky man," though they still get along well.

One evening during the Durban Test in 1994 several of the South African players, including Hansie Cronje, Andrew Hudson and Rhodes, led a prayer rally. Jonty came out the next day and had a lot of luck and his good fortune peaked when Boon held what we thought was a catch at short leg, but Boonie said it did not carry.

AB walked past Jonty and said to him, "Can you tell me when the next rally is on ... I'll be there."

In a Test in Cape Town in 1994 I watched the South Africans bat in the nets during the match before play and they were simply slogging everything, which was quite surprising because they were in a desperate predicament in the match and should have been focusing on nothing more than survival. When Brian McMillan came out to bat I said quite loudly within earshot of him, "We are going to have to bowl very well here, because I saw him at net practice this morning and he was hitting it everywhere."

Next over I said, "We aren't going too badly. Brian is one of my favourite players and we are keeping him scoreless."

As soon as I mentioned how Brian had a blitz in the nets he went into his shell. We got him out soon after lbw to Steve Waugh for three and won the Test.

In the next Test at Durban, when I was batting he said to me, "You know, Heals, you are one of my very favourite players," which I accepted as a little victory in the verbal stakes, because it meant my initial chip had got through to him and was still on his mind.

Fanie de Villiers' mental strength was evident during a "team building" exercise he once put his South African team-mates through. It involved players forming a circle and punching the player immediately to their right. The boys enjoyed it to a degree because the player who you punched never got the chance to return the blow, so some players were letting fly knowing their victim could not retaliate. Then, to everyone's surprise, Fanie called, "Okay, now we will change direction," and some of the players reputedly couldn't go through with it, petrified that they could get critically wounded.

Of course the little arrows don't always work and can occasionally rebound on your side.

In a Test in Sri Lanka in 1992 Asanka Gurusinha repeatedly played and missed when he tried to work Greg Matthews across the line through mid-wicket. I said to him, "Any danger of playing straight?" so he started playing straight and cleaned us up.

Mark Taylor overheard my comment and later said, "Any danger of you shutting your mouth."

In my diaries I have a small saying which goes, "Be the master of body language, the detector of none." The master of this was Richards, who, through his gum-chewing, half-smiling, super-cool demeanour on the cricket field,

Few cricketers have radiated such an imposing aura as 'The Master Blaster',
Viv Richards. I'm celebrating his demise, bowled by Peter Taylor in a one-day
international in Jamaica, 1991.

Opposite page: *A constant barrage of short-pitched fast bowling can weaken*
the resolve, break the spirit. It's called intimidation, and the West Indies knew
how to do it best.

GREGG PORTEOUS/NEWS LTD

radiated the belief that he was feeling pretty damn good about himself in any situation—an aura of invincibility. It seemed his sense of self-belief ran so deep he was immune to the body language and the strength of others. Barring his confrontations with Tugga, Viv was so self-absorbed it always looked as if he didn't know or care whether his rivals were even on the field.

Yet when you spend five minutes in his company you know he is just like you or me. Getting behind the mask is an important element of cricket or any sport.

The West Indian fast bowlers of my era, and those which preceded it, could sniff out body language better than any team. Any slight sign of nerves or a weak heart and they lifted a cog to be all over the batsman with their body-seeking missiles.

Over the years many West Indian fast bowlers have deliberately not mixed socially with their opponents, because they like to keep their enigmatic aura about them.

The two exceptions were Michael Holding and Joel Garner but they were good enough to get away with touching glasses with a rival one evening, then touching his helmet with a thunderbolt the next day.

And the big thing about them is that they were always consistent mixers. Opposition sides never had the luxury of thinking, "Michael hasn't been in for a drink for a while ... must be feeling the pressure." He was always socialising and consequently maintaining the impression he had everything in hand. As Australian audiences know, he normally did.

One of my great goals in cricket is to be regarded as a bloke who will never be run over by anyone. They might get me one day, but the next day I want to be as hard to climb over as ever.

My top mental tough nuts of cricket are:

STEVE WAUGH
A clever exponent of the mind game, both serving and receiving. While using the taunts of others to his advantage, he knows how to chip away at other players and put them off their game.

This is one of the reasons he has gained such useful returns from his medium pace in Test cricket. He has a distracting aura about him at the bowling crease and Carl Hooper, who has fallen to Steve five times in Tests, is just one big-name player to be put off his game.

Tugga works at distracting the batsman and getting himself into a position of control. He fancies himself against Lara—it's an ego thing because if someone like Waugh stares at Lara, Brian wants to give it back. Tugga adopted the same theory when he bounced Viv Richards, for the 'Master Blaster' had such a huge ego he would not tolerate being bounced by a medium pacer and would attempt to fire back harder than ever.

But Tugga has had several memorable successes. The favourite stumping of my career, Graeme Thorpe at Edgbaston in 1993, came off a wide Shane Warne wrong 'un which spun away from the left-hander and involved a wide sweep of the gloves—after a splash of gamesmanship. Wickets were tumbling to such an extent it appeared Thorpe could have been stranded not out at the end of the innings. Tugga, stationed several metres from the batsman, worked beautifully on Thorpe's temperament when he said to me within earshot of the batsman, "This bloke will be concentrating on getting red ink ... he will want to be not out and won't want to face Warne." Totally out of character, and as if to say "I'll show you blokes", Thorpe charged Warne next ball and missed, his first big stroke of the innings.

I have never been associated with a sportsman who thinks so positively. Mentally he is just indomitable and I try to emulate him. He tends to pull his team-mates up along the same direction.

JAVED MIANDAD

On my first tour of Pakistan in 1988, Miandad was the centre of a storm of controversy over the rejection of no fewer than five lbw appeals. It made about as much impression on him as a rain drop on a tiled roof. A lesser temperament might have felt a bit guilty and taken it a bit easier, thinking, "I should have been out ages ago." Javed has enormous mental strength and an insatiable appetite for runs. Sledging just doesn't bother him—he gives the impression he thrives on it. He accepts pressure and turns it back on other people—a precious skill, in my view. At Sabina Park, Jamaica, one of the game's most hostile cauldrons, West Indian Ken Benjamin was running through the crease to bowl bouncers at Javed from about 18 metres when Javed decided enough was enough. He charged down the pitch, pointed to his own chin and shouted, "Here it is ... see if you are good enough to hit it."

RICHARD HADLEE

Like Richards, De villiers and Boon he was a master at concealing his inner thoughts. Hadlee could've lost the family fortune a hour before play and had a car accident on the way to the ground but you would never have noticed from the way he hustled back to his mark with his businesslike stride, which had contained as much spring in dire demanding days in India and Pakistan as it did in the more friendly surrounds of New Zealand and England.

Cricket is a team game, and few cricketers have ever held such a sway over their team's fortunes as Hadlee.

For more than a decade he was the first choice and the last resort, the man in the middle on whom everything depended for New Zealand cricket.

Yet he never let his country, county, or himself down ... even though the game once drove him to the brink of a nervous breakdown.

As an allrounder who finds it hard to fire as a 'keeper and batsman during the one period, I admire Hadlee's effort to average 50 with the bat and beneath 20 with the ball for Nottinghamshire in county cricket in the one season.

He had a great awareness of his own game which he kept refining and tinkering with until it became near perfect.

He squeezed every last drop out of his potential by relentless analysis, not only of himself but of those who he could learn from, like Dennis Lillee. He kept diaries on rival players and though he was a self-made champion, he always had an ear for a helpful tip.

When Hadlee was in India chasing the wicket that would make him the world record holder for most Test victims, wicket-keeper Ian Smith called him down the pitch after his first two overs.

Smithy pointed to a series of red marks left just short of a length on the pitch and said, "Richard, look at these ... you won't get that wicket unless you are hitting the deck another two metres on."

Hadlee immediately took the advice on board and got his wicket next over by pitching the ball to where the 'keeper had pointed.

And, in another great show of mental strength and supreme faith in his ability, he boldly branded Dean Jones his bunny midway through his last Test series in Australia.

"I've got the wood on Dean Jones," he trumpeted in a column he wrote. In days of super-conservative public statements where no-one likes to set themselves up for a fall, it was a brave move.

ALLAN BORDER

I won't dwell here on Allan (who will be discussed at length in THE BOYS chapter) but I rate him as one of the toughest nuts.

DICING
WITH DESI

*"I like competitive cricketers, people who give their all.
Healy is like that."*

DESMOND HAYNES

There was plenty of good blood spilt and bad blood circulating in Australia's volatile clash with the West Indies in the Caribbean in 1991.

The contest was labelled at the time as the most acrimonious tour since Bodyline—there were at least five visits by players from both sides to hospital, savage verbal exchanges both on and off the field, controversial and at times flawed umpiring decisions and a frustrating manipulation of the 90-over per day rule.

The "Healy headline" was my infamous first day stoush with Desmond Haynes in the Fourth Test in Barbados, Haynes' home town.

This had its origins in a one-day match in Guyana where I was left puzzled by a disagreement with Haynes. Haynes was out lbw to Peter Taylor in Guyana and as I walked past him to celebrate with the bowler Desmond gave me the cold stare of a man with plenty on his mind—and I got the impression the venomous thoughts were mostly about yours truly.

I said nothing as Haynes walked away, but when Mark Waugh arrived from the outfield he said, "What did you say to Desi? He's into you. He said 'Tell Healy he is a thief.'"

Later, when we batted, Allan Border took full advantage of a ball that had slipped out of Phil Simmons' hand and skewed out of control onto a neighbouring pitch ... a free hit.

You don't get too many free hits in the Caribbean and AB's eyes widened like a kid who's just seen Santa come out of the chimney, and he darted across and belted the ball for six.

Haynes was unimpressed and sailed into AB, accusing him of showing disregard for the spirit of the game, and what followed was what you'd call a "a sharp verbal exchange". Bruce Reid, our acting 12th man, was called into the war-zone at the height of ill feeling and I can still hear him saying upon his return to the dressing room, "Wow, there's plenty happening out there between AB and Haynes."

At the presentation after stumps Haynes asked Mark Waugh whether he passed the "thief" message on to me and Junior replied, "Yes, what's your problem?" But the simple fact was I needed to confront Haynes myself, to find out what it was all about, and, determined to bring the issue to a head I took off into the West Indies room with two cold beers and Dean Jones.

Heads craned everywhere as we walked in. Haynes refused to take my beer, grabbed one of his own, then revealed the problem was what he considered to be my excessive appealing.

He said the more times I appealed the more chance I had of getting an unfair decision that went against his side.

I replied, "But Desi, you were given out. What's your problem?"

He added, "Yes but there have been plenty of times when you have been appealing and they weren't out."

It was quite a sharp-edged conversation. I was interested to read in Haynes' biography, *The Lion of Barbados* (in which I'm described as the provocative 'keeper with the weaselly smile) Haynes claiming he did not believe he got through to me in that conversation.

That's true—neither of us could crash through each other's self-righteous defences. We were both so busy trying to force-feed each other with our stance on the matter we didn't bother listening to what the other party had to say. I knew he wasn't listening to me because the answers I was getting were unrelated to the questions I was asking. In fact, it briefly took me back to my teaching days at Kingston High School.

Gordon Greenidge, speaking more than I have heard him before or since, was chipping in from the bleachers with the odd word of support for Haynes. I felt I wasn't getting anywhere, so I walked out.

My philosophy on appealing has changed and mellowed over the years. When I first entered the Australian team, I was criticised for the regularity and over-exuberance of my appeals.

The fact that we were a battling side shaped my conduct, because I wanted the bowlers to think there was plenty of support for them. It wasn't hard to stay keyed up about appealing because next to me at first slip was Terry Alderman, who expected my voice to reach a decibel level normally achieved by Jimmy Barnes when I appealed off his bowling.

At the end of an over, if I had not shown great keenness in an appeal, Terry would often say, "What was that bloody missing?" or "Where were you when I needed you?"

So I promised myself I would not miss a chance, but what I lacked was an awareness of how other people were perceiving it. I gradually came to notice television commentators were branding me as over-exuberant, but I

No goats in this Caribbean practice session, just some inquisitive locals.

*The day I stumped the boys! I told them it was a novel fielding drill, and even
had 'The Colonel', Lawrie Sawle mark their performance, but in reality it was
just the old, head-down-spin-around-the-stump trick, and when they tried to return
to the starting point most lost their bearings—naturally!*

was prepared to ignore their criticism so long as I was doing the right thing by the team.

These days I feel more confident about coping with a bowler's vented spleen and have no problems saying, "Mate, I thought it was missing leg."

The incident in the Fourth Test at Barbados flared when Haynes snicked a Craig McDermott off-cutter onto his pad—I am sure he hit it—and I lunged down the leg-side to catch it. The West Indies would have been 4–28, with Haynes out for 10, had the decision fallen our way. It was an absolutely crucial verdict.

Haynes gestured that the ball had come from his hip, which angered me. There are several players in the world—India's Manoj Prabarkar is one—who really get up my nose by signalling to the umpire that the ball has come off bat when the opposition is appealing for an lbw. Or when the appeal is for a catch behind they promptly signal it hit their pad shirt, or any other garment within range.

So Desi, fresh from his little "Don't you dare try and influence the umpire" sermon in Guyana and with his saintly halo firmly in place, was engaging in a little bit of brinkmanship that I found quite hard to swallow. He was trying to do exactly what he told me not to do ... unfairly influence the umpire.

Mustering all the subtlety that I am renowned for, I said to him, "Why don't you let the f---ing umpire do his f---ing job."

At this point he took his helmet off and walked slowly towards me, bat cocked in a horizontal plane above his right shoulder, prodded in my direction as if he was about to poke me in the chest. He said, "I don't have to take that from you."

I said, "You have to take what you get out here, mate."

He shot back with, "How about I see you after the game?" which drew a terse reply of "You are a big man, aren't you?" from me and I blew him a kiss and went back to my position.

Haynes batted for 212 minutes that day for 28, an incredibly slow knock by his standards, but you could see he just wanted to stick it into us after the early exchange.

At the lunch break, manager Laurie Sawle and coach Bob Simpson sought me out, wanting to know what I had said. After telling them what had happened I felt quite comfortable when Simmo said, "That's been happening in cricket for 50 years."

Simpson leapt to my defence when grilled by the press after I refused to comment. He said, "It's rather unusual to see a batsman come to a wicket-keeper in a situation like that and continue the onslaught as he leaves the field. From what I understand, nothing was said on the field to warrant that sort of reaction. I am happy with Healy's behaviour and cannot understand

*My dice with Desi on the 1991
Caribbean tour. Photographer Gregg
Porteous didn't miss a syllable!*

the reason for Haynes' over-reaction."

I sensed they felt there must have been more to the argument, but I felt vindicated the next day when the text of the argument was printed in the local papers after Haynes held a press conference. He told Barbados' *Sunday Sun*, "Healy used abusive language at me and I am sorry if it looked as if I was protesting because he appealed. It was just a matter of showing Healy where the ball hit me on my shirt, but then he started cursing me.

"It was not that I was trying in any way to make a scene and I apologise to the fans and people of Barbados."

Later he added, "I was in Barbados, my home, in front of my people and that made it harder to take and easier to snap back."

No Australian got along with Haynes throughout the entire series. A lasting image is of him standing with a towel over his bowed head at the presentation ceremony following the last Test.

The Barbados incident spotlighted the increasing tension between two sides in a sour, ill-tempered series and stirred up the local faithful who rallied strongly behind their man.

I really battled in the field after the incident, and was given an insight into the depth of their emotion in the bus on the way home. As the bus weaved through the tiny impoverished streets of Bridgetown on a well-used route to the team motel, several locals stood waiting in their front yards and waved their fists at me.

The clash sparked pleas for calm by former players who had been around in the days when the two teams had shared a harmonious relationship. Wes Hall even took Haynes aside to try to persuade him to shed his confrontational demeanour. "I told him that as vice-captain he was setting a bad example," Wes said. "I told him what I thought because he is a good fellow and he wouldn't like something like this to tarnish his name. I think I got the message through to him. I accept he was upset and the incident may have looked worse than what it was, but when you go around lifting your bat and taking your helmet off you tend to get noticed.

"What annoys me is that I have played cricket all around the world and I inadvertently have busted more heads and hands than any other fast bowler. But I have not met anyone who played against me in 30 years who is not my friend. I wouldn't like to think that Desmond or other West Indian players will spoil their chances of enjoying their retirement with similar friendships because of a few silly incidents at this stage of their careers."

The Haynes incident had a peaceful punchline when Desi, reflecting on it five years later, told the *Sydney Morning Herald* he had no grudges.

He said, "You cannot have something happen on a cricket field then go on holding animosity towards anyone. You can't hold grudges because the game goes on. There's a lot of life after cricket.

"In Ian's first couple of years against us I felt he was trying to put a bit of pressure on the umpire by appealing for everything. I guess sometimes that works. The guys' a good 'keeper and that is that.

"What I like about him as a 'keeper is that he keeps the fielders going. He gives the team that bit of inspiration. I like competitive cricketers, people who give their all. Healy is like that."

The following summer Channel Nine used a clip of my exchange with Haynes to promote their cricket coverage and I protested to our management, feeling it was a case of double standards from cricket to be baking me for misbehaving then using my performance to promote the game.

Channel Nine argued they had paid for the pictures, could do what they wanted with them and had no obligation to serve the interests of the ACB. With hindsight I now understand their position.

I was an angry man after the Bardabos Test for a multitude of reasons. How we managed to lose the match by 343 runs after bowling out the West Indies for 149 in their first innings is beyond me.

We collapsed for 134 in our first innings then the home side amassed 536. Commentator Tony Cozier did not do our cause much of a favour by writing that Gordon Greenidge was all but finished as a Test batsman—he made 226.

My seething state of mind after the Barbados Test was evident with this vitriolic entry in my diary:

This game was extremely frustrating due to:

(1) The West Indies' pettiness and denial of everything.
(2) Their rush to the media with our faults.
(3) Their aggression and basic hatred which seems to be allowed to go unchecked.
(4) Pitiful standard of umpiring.

We rebounded to win the last Test in Antigua to finish 1–2 down in the series. But on reflection I still wonder whether deep down we really had the inner belief needed to beat the West Indies at home. One curiously lax day's cricket in the Third Test in Trinidad is a case in point. In a rain-affected game, we made 294 then steamed through the West Indies to have them 7–110 on the fourth day.

The chances of a result were not great but at the very point when we should have been wheeling in the cannons and mortar guns, our attack became curiously circumspect.

We bowled absolute rubbish to Curtly Ambrose who made 55 and, together with Jeff Dujon (70) gave the Windies a safe passage to a draw.

I wrote in my diary:

"No continuous pressure on batsmen ... almost as if we didn't want to annihilate them ... instead we just wanted to bat for a draw ... less pressure that way ... DO WE WANT TO NAIL THESE BLOKES?"

That series featured our last sighting of the great Malcolm Marshall, the best West Indian fast bowler I've faced. For all of Ambrose's exceptional qualities I rate Marshall top of the pile. He simply had everything ... pace when he needed it, the ability to bowl on dead wickets, to toil through long spells, to swing the ball both ways, to bowl a good bouncer, to rarely get hit.

I am quite relieved I did not have to face him at his peak.

Ah, the wonders of modern technology. No sooner had Helen given birth to Emma than she had in her spare hand a photo of me celebrating on the other side of the world. It was 26 February 1991, and I was in Jamaica.

JAMIE HANSEN/COURIER-MAIL

WORLD
CHAMPIONS

"We can take these blokes down today."

STEVE WAUGH, KINGSTON, JAMAICA, 1 MAY 1995

Australia's 157 run win against the West Indies in the Fifth Test in Antigua in 1991 may not have made a massive imprint on the cricket world, but it was a significant step towards Australia becoming world champions in 1995.

It was the final Test of the series and effectively a dead match, because the West Indies had already annexed the series 2–0.

It was a tough, at times vicious, series. To finish it with a Test match win left us craving more success and gave us a sense of unfinished duty; we knew we were assembling a side capable of winning The Frank Worrell Trophy.

Then, in 1992–93 we had been denied a victory by one run in Adelaide, a victory that would have seen us go to an unbeatable 2–0 series lead. Instead the series was tied up and then lost in demoralising circumstances in Perth. Stumps had barely been drawn at Perth when our minds starting plotting for revenge in the West Indies in 1995.

It wasn't done in a big way, just dressing room banter, subtle experimentation and occasional planning.

Just before we left for the Caribbean, Steve Waugh summed up the thoughts of a few of the players by saying, "There's a group of players here who have grown up together. Beating the Windies is something we have always wanted to do and after this series we may be split up and never get the chance to do it together.

"It has to be done now and I think we've got the team to do it."

Although we lost the one-day series 4–1 no-one thought this meant our Test campaign was shot down. Mark Taylor had said the one-day series was a low priority—"Let's use the one-dayers as a lead-up—no-one remembers them." In some ways I became frustrated with our approach, because it disappointed me to see us under-achieve. I felt we could have won both series.

But Taylor's approach would later prove to be a masterstroke.

A tour of the West Indies has not officially started until there has been a major travel hitch and I was one of the unsuspecting victims of our first major stuff-up of the tour.

We were leaving St Vincent for Guyana via Trinidad, when, in the boarding lounge of the St Vincent airport, someone said it seemed odd we were not issued with boarding passes. It transpired that the airline we were travelling with had reduced the boarding proceeding to the equivalent of a flag race at a beach carnival by booking 41 passengers for 37 seats.

Sadly, scorer Mike Walsh, Warnie, manager Jack Edwards and myself were unaware of the numbers game and missed out as we were the last four on the plane.

Someone told Jack there was a seat in the front of the plane and he said, "Good, that'll do me" while myself, Shane and Walshie reluctantly left the plane to catch a charter flight.

We arrived in Guyana seven hours after the remainder of the party. Our pilot on the nine-seater charter flight laughed at us as we got onto the plane, claiming "You don't get this for murder."

He was referring to the fact that the noise level of the plane was like being on the inside of a motor mower.

The three of us were dirty and depressed when we landed in Guyana. Poor old Jack, our manager, became a marked man as we said things like, "When Jack turns up at the airport to pick us up he will get a gobful ... and if he doesn't pick us up we will give him an even bigger gobful."

Jack took the later option and you can imagine our spirits after the hour long bus trip, when we walked into the motel and the boys started laughing at us from the bar. Jack just raised his glass and invited us to come and have a drink.

Out of the seeds of our disappointment in the 1992–93 series sprung a united resolve to trade them punch for punch, thunderbolt for thunderbolt in the next series. Our collective state of mind was: "Bugger it ... we are sick of copping it. It is time to have a go back at them." Tubsy spelt out precisely to the bowlers what was expected of them and how he expected them to bowl against the West Indies. Part of that plan was to show no respect to their tail-end batsmen. Glenn McGrath was the perfect man to bounce their tail, for on the field he is a fearless character with a mean streak who couldn't care what the Windies dished out to him in return.

We call him Norman or Batesy after Norman Bates in the movie *Psycho*. His bowling in this series was equal to the fastest I have 'kept to and as fast as anything the West Indies could manage.

And we had separate plans for each batsman, as usual: Sherwin Campbell is a big leg-side player so the obvious plan was to bowl outside off-stump. Stuart Williams is a big shot-maker who hates being tied down; pressure most likely would yield a rash stroke. Brian Lara: anything on his legs tends to

In a party mood after the win at Sabina Park.

disappear, but he often flashes at wide balls—chance of a catch to gully. Carl Hooper likes to score quickly but gets out in the simplest ways when tied down. Richie Richardson, murderous on anything outside off-stump, so the ball must be angled into off-stump.

Our planning even went as far as bouncing our own batsmen in the nets at the start of the tour. There were some fearsome deliveries unleashed in the nets in Barbados in our early tour practice sessions—a dose of medicine which might taste bad at the time but had great long-term benefit. No other Australian side I had played with had tried this tactic before.

Then, tragedy. In 1991 in the Caribbean Hughes and McDermott had bowled with great aggression against the Windies but we lacked a third bowler. I'm sure if Bruce Reid had been fit we would have won the series. Now, on this tour all our planning threatened to fall apart when Craig McDermott and Damien Fleming were sent home injured and we were fielding one of our most inexperienced pace attacks for decades.

The Test series started on a frantic, pulsating note in Barbados when we reduced them to 3–6 after Williams, Campbell and Richardson were all back in the pavilion, but in a fascinating session of punch and counter punch, Carl Hooper proceeded to charge Warne and, with Lara, had resuscitated the innings to a respectable 3–116 at lunch.

Soon after lunch, Lara, on 65, smashed a widish Julian outswinger to Steve Waugh in the gully. Waugh clutched at it and the ball bobbled out of his hands as he tumbled towards the turf. Steve had another two attempts at catching it before it came to rest on top of his left wrist. He at last grabbed it and tossed it skyward.

The unusual thing about the Waugh catch was that none of the players were aware there was a problem until the end of the day. But after stumps Simmo asked Tugga, "What are you going to say to the press?" and Tugga replied with something like "About what?" Normally when a major controversy occurs the players will know what will be on the back page tomorrow. The slips thought he had taken a fair catch and so did I.

My verdict was that the videos were inconclusive. And anyway I didn't look at it too hard because I had nothing to do with it, and I didn't need the hassles.

With 4–64 in that innings, Brendon Julian paid his way for the series. One suspects BJ will always be something of an enigma. When he is on song he is a tremendous bowler. When he loses control he gets down on himself.

There were a few early signals in that Test that the brick wall of West Indies cricket was about to come tumbling down.

The first came while I was batting. I came to the wicket at 5–194, one behind the West Indies first innings total, and made 74 not out as we hustled to 346, a lead of 151.

Every run hurt them and I noted, with glee, their lack of chatter and encouragement for the bowlers. The further we pressed ahead the quieter they became in the field.

You could tell they were hoping for a wicket rather than expecting one.

Then when they batted, Courtney Walsh was bounced by Glenn McGrath and his emotions went haywire. Courtney has been known to play-act at the crease, but he simply lost the plot under pressure in the first innings.

He playfully ran down the pitch towards McGrath, as if pretending to challenge him, then he would race off towards square leg. He was out of control. Even his helmet wasn't properly fastened. He looked like a man under extreme pressure.

Another sign the Windies had changed character came in the opening overs of their second innings. At stumps on day two they had crept to 0–15 off 13 overs.

In the old days, you could bowl the West Indies out for under 300 once in a game but never twice. They rebounded like a rubber ball and would come at you harder than ever. But it struck me on that second afternoon that this West Indian team didn't know how to play the old West Indian way. A deficit of 151 had made them nervous. It was all in their body language.

Even their approach to Warnie had become instantly cautious. Hooper tried to belt him in the first innings, got out, and never tried it again all series. Nor did the rest of them.

The entire Australian team left the field that night thinking all we had to do was bowl tightly and they would self-destruct. And they did.

The Windies mustered only 189 in their second innings and their strained emotions were evident as we rushed to victory by posting 0–39 off 6.5 overs. Walsh and Kenny Benjamin went through the crease—the back foot was where the front foot would normally be, placing them much closer to the batsmen when they let go vicious bouncers. Benjamin's was so wild it gave us victory via extras.

Any Test victory is a proud moment but this one was especially emotional given the setbacks we had to endure and how convincingly we won.

Our match winning team song was sung with great passion and minutes later the strains of "Waltzing Matilda" and "Advance Australia Fair" came through the dressing room windows as our supporters were in hearty voice.

No sooner had we inflicted a few wounds on the West Indies than the local press were queuing up with much sharper instruments. They accused the side of too much socialising and not enough motivation and demanded the head of captain Richie Richardson.

Richie was berated as being dull and unimaginative and the effort was rated by one critic as "a gutless surrender".

Richie Richardson was always under pressure.

GREGG PORTEOUS/ NEWS LTD

The Second Test in Antigua was a provocative teaser because rain before lunch on the last day ended it in a draw, but it provided further evidence that the West Indies' confidence was on the wane. Before a ball had been bowled there was massive conjecture in the press over whether the Windies should bat or bowl if they won a toss on a pitch that looked as if it could be useful to the fast men early.

And it got back to us that there were conflicting views in the West Indian camp. Even when the coin fell his way at the toss, Richardson dwelt for a moment or two before saying, "We'll bowl."

It struck me then that suddenly after all these years of dominance the West Indies had to put a great deal of thought into their tactics. Unlike previous captains, Richardson no longer had the luxury of knowing that if he bowled first he was all but certain to know his bowlers would vindicate the decision and if he batted, his top order would be in the runs. Both departments were showing signs of frailty.

The Third Test was in Trinidad, and assessing the pitch was not difficult, the main problem was finding it! The grass was more than two centimetres long and it was moist—a fast bowler's delight. It was in such an underprepared state that on match morning I asked Tubsy, "Are we going to start on time?"

The pitch needed at least another day to be up to Test standard. Tight, low-scoring Tests can provide gripping entertainment and an invigorating challenge. I am not totally against the odd seaming wicket, though this one was probably too far in favour of the bowlers. Simmo summed it up well, saying, "When a wicket seams like that you won't get runs consistently no matter whether you are Brian Lara or Don Bradman."

The other facet of it is that it demeans the effort of great fast bowlers, because lesser tradesmen can be just as effective simply by putting the ball on the spot and letting the wicket do the work.

Tugga plugged away brilliantly, and with a bit of good fortune, to make 63 not out. He was hammered mercilessly and even traded words with Ambrose from three metres, who was baited by Steve and responded with, "Don't you cuss me, man."

Occasionally in Test cricket you get a hunch about the way an evenly poised game will fall and we sensed this was ours for the taking at stumps on the second day when we were 0–20, effectively 0–8.

The Windies had launched a merciless assault of short-pitched bowling at Slater and Taylor, who later wrote in his book, *Taylor Made*, "I've been hit from pillar to post. If it wasn't intimidatory bowling then I am a bad judge. I faced around 45 balls and somewhere between 20 and 30 of them were short-pitched. It wasn't cricket. I don't think people know what intimidatory bowling is anymore."

Steve Waugh's direct hit runs out Richie Richardson in the first one-day international.

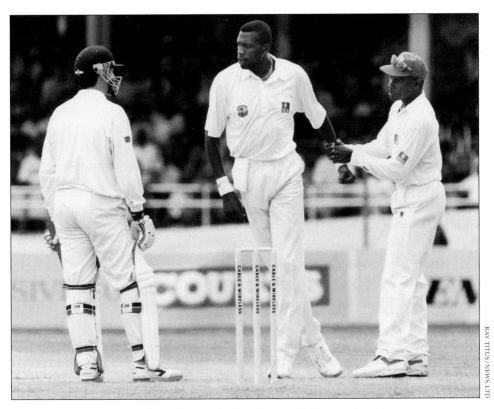

Steve Waugh and Curtly Ambrose have a difference of opinion.

We had tumbled into the abyss on the first day, scrambled our way out on the second, and series glory would surely be ours on the third.

Or so we thought. We picked a poor time to have a shocker, tumbling for 105 and losing our last seven wickets for 20. Ambrose took four and the pitch was only partially to blame. I believe our problem in the second innings can be traced to our plan to try to bat the entire day to put the game beyond the West Indies' reach. Under the circumstances, it just wasn't a practical goal. The Windies rattled off the 98 needed for victory in quick time. So we went to Jamaica for the last Test one-all.

The totally bare Jamaican strip was rolled and polished to give it the sheen of a dance room floor. Its appearance generated a quip among the boys that Mark Waugh had no chance of succeeding—because he would spend most of his time looking at his reflection in the pitch.

We got a signal that Tubby had lost his fourth toss in a row—not from Tubby but from four groundsmen standing nearby, raising their arms triumphantly when Richie won first bat on a belter.

'Keeping to Warne on a pitch that had become crumbling and ugly when the Jamaica Test was drawing to its mighty conclusion became so difficult and dangerous that Tubby Taylor suggested I don a helmet. One ball had spat from the crumbling pitch and gone over my head while another went through my legs.

Tubby said he was concerned that if I became injured someone else would have to 'keep to Warnie under the most trying of circumstances and might not be up to the task, risking further injury.

I thought it wasn't a bad idea and found 'keeping in a helmet was not uncomfortable. It probably should be done more often, though it would be useful to develop a lighter model.

We rolled them for 265 and then sat back and watched the greatest partnership and individual innings I have seen. Tugga Waugh's 200 is one of those knocks which was destined to become a landmark in Australian cricket history from the day he constructed it. He shared a stand of 231 with brother Mark who scored 126.

Steve batted for close on 10 hours, faced 425 balls and surely at least 200 of these had to be short-pitched. At the sponsors function at the end of the third day he could barely hold a drink cup, for he had several nasty fingers.

As I watched him running between wickets I thought, "Here's a bloke who wouldn't run 400 metres if you offered him a new car, yet he's taking off like the wind, ducking and dodging like a boxer and showing remarkable fitness and energy."

Steve is among the most positive of players. When he came into the dressing room during breaks in play during his innings he would say, "These blokes are going down today."

A rare photo, the Waugh twins posing together—and almost touching!

He was almost in a trance-like state in the dressing room, though when Justin Langer asked how he was feeling, Steve replied, "I've never felt better or more comfortable."

The Waugh boys found the Jamaican wicket hard and bouncy, just like the WACA strip where they have had so much success. The West Indies probably overdid the short ball to Tugga. He might not have looked pretty playing it, but he was mightily effective, as evidenced by the fact that neither Ambrose nor Walsh got him out all series.

The thing about the short ball is that it may cause discomfort for a while, but once a top batsmen is used to it he simply gets the feeling it is not going to get him out. That's what happened to Tugga that day and, indeed, that series.

The West Indies had no plan B. Steve advanced to his double century late on day three and was an exhausted figure after stumps. He wanted a beer but Carl Rackemann refused to give him one, instead thrusting a Coke in his hand. Steve was mystified by the gesture until he tasted it. Big Carl, the most thoughtful of tourists, had tracked down a bottle of Tugga's favourite drink, Southern Comfort, and had poured him a Southern and Coke.

Steve had provided an innings Australia would always cherish. I know Queenslanders still appreciate it, because a year after the innings Steve gave a pair of his gloves used in that innings for auction at Dirk Tazelaar's Testimonial night and they raised $1750.

Fittingly Mark Taylor took the catch that sealed our victory, pocketed the ball and later handed it as a souvenir to Simmo, whose quest to beat the West Indies had started a decade before.

The dressing room was in a state of chaos, cameras were firing, champagne was spurting.

We took the Frank Worrell Trophy back on the bus to the team hotel as one of the younger members of the party held up his glass and roared, "Cheers to Frank Worrell ... whoever he is."

The celebrations that night lingered on to 4am at the hotel. Justin Langer was still draped in an Australian flag, but my last and favourite image was of Steve Waugh still in his creams, spikes and green cap despite the fact that the sun would rise in another hour, walking in that Charlie Chaplin way of his down the corridor. He was looking very closely at each door number until he found his.

Appropriately it was room 200, a sweet reminder of the innings that placed Australia on top of the cricket world.

THE SIMPSON ERA

"I shall stay the way I am because I do not give a damn."
DOROTHY PARKER

If you had to rate a cricket person out of 10 for sheer love of the game, then Australian cricket would have two 11s—Bob Simpson and Allan Border.

Simpson deserves a gold medal from the Australian Cricket Board for the amount of his life he's poured into the game in this country. I estimate he has devoted more than 40 years to Australian cricket as a player, coach and selector and the game was the better for it. Simmo's enthusiasm for the game was quite incredible. On big days, such as the first day of a Test match or a one-day final, he would be dressed and bounding about as if he would be playing in the game. He simply loved it.

Some great players can excel in the sport for a decade without being able to fully understand the intricacies of their craft. Simpson was not one of these. He was quite exceptional at spotting a fault and rectifying it, technically and mentally.

Small observations can yield mighty dividends in Test cricket. After the 1991 West Indies tour Simpson privately pointed out to David Boon that he'd slipped into a mental comfort zone, a result of being a permanent member of the side. Simmo felt Boon's security had subconsciously reduced his hunger for runs. It was a subtle spur that propelled Boon to the top of the Australian averages for the next few summers, which yielded the greatest form of his career. And Boon's exceptional progress at short leg was Simmo driven.

In 1991 Simmo wrote down a piece of advice to me I considered so worthwhile I put it in the front of my yearly diary. He wrote, "Further improve your batting horizons. So far only a small part of your talent has been exposed. I still feel your self-destruct button gets pushed too frequently. It is almost as if you accelerate into disaster and if you get 4, 5 or 6 per over you can't get off the roller coaster. This continued acceleration ends in dismissal. Once you learn to control that aspect of your batting you will score Test 100s.

You must never repress completely your natural aggression, just temper it with a higher level of commonsense and calm.

No use getting the shits after the dismissal; more control and composure before the act is a greater way to success."

Before our triumphant West Indies tour of 1995 Simpson worked on helping Steve Waugh turn short balls off his body down to fine leg rather than just drop them at his feet. Simpson saw this as imperative for Waugh, because he did not pull or hook and simply had to find some way of scoring runs off the squillion short balls he was always going to receive in that series. It worked, for Steve was man of the series and a large source of runs came from tucks around the corner.

Geoff Marsh, who has taken over from Simmo, reportedly was a very hard-handed fieldsman before Simpson converted him into a glue-fingered champion in the gully.

In the 1987 World Cup Simmo instructed Mike Veletta to charge opposition bowlers not by backing away but by moving straight at them, which opened up scoring opportunities on both sides of the wicket. Veletta was one of the finds of the tournament—which Australia won—and his dare-devil tactics confounded opposition captains, who found it almost impossible to set a containing field to him.

Simpson must also take some credit for improving the batting skills of the bowlers, who he ensured had quality time in the nets. Merv Hughes was such a poor batsman in a Test career launched with three ducks he once listed his goal in cricket was "to score a Test match run". Merv eventually made 1032 runs at an average of almost 17 and no doubt a portion of his improvement can be attributed to the coach's efforts.

Players often took Simmo's coaching for granted. When asked to name the greatest influence on their career, they'd often mention their boyhood coach who'd tutored them for one or two years rather than the man who helped to shape their international success for over half a decade.

If we were to be as honest as we should be, Simpson had to be one of the greatest influences on all of us.

Simmo played mind games better than a cold war general and could play one against the other with great aplomb, but none of that really worried me. If you were totally honest with him you had nothing to worry about. I believe he was much more even handed than he's been given credit for.

But he did have trouble establishing smooth rapport with a lot of players. Some found it hard to be up front with him, and often never really knew where they stood with him.

There was a major communications gap between Simpson and many players who came into the Australian side in the mid-'80s because, rightly or wrongly, Simpson was seen as the one who truncated the international careers of players like Wayne Phillips, Greg Ritchie and Tim Zoehrer. This intimidated some players and consequently their chances of having a prosperous relationship with Simmo were reduced.

There was a distance between Simmo and the player, so free-flowing chats,

When 'keeping wicket got downright dangerous, and the bowler wasn't even quick—he was Shane Warne. The pitch had started to break up on the last day of the Fourth Test at Sabina Park, Jamaica, when we clinched the Frank Worrell Trophy, creating variable bounce. My captain Mark Taylor said, "Get a helmet!"

Opposite page: *Bad luck, Keith. One of the sweetest dismissals—Keith Arthurton leg before to Warnie in the Frank Worrell Trophy deciding Fourth Test in Jamaica in 1995.*

Previous page: *The West Indies call it "getting on the stepladder". I'm a couple of rungs up during the 1995 tour to the Caribbean—but even though my feet are off the ground my eyes are still on the ball!*

Skittled by Curtly Ambrose on a green top in Trinidad.

OK, I know it's only small, but ... we had bigger fish to fry in the Caribbean in 1995!

Previous pages: *A practice session with a difference in the Caribbean.*

The new world champions celebrate ... after the victory in Jamaica we "let down", with wives and girlfriends, in Bermuda; cigars for me, Justin Langer, Steve Waugh and Carl Rackemann, then full throttle on mopeds around the island.

*Captain and vice-captain,
and the spoils of victory.*

Simmo throwing himself into another fielding practice session.

where the coach firmly states what is expected and a player pours out his inner thoughts, were significantly absent. I don't entirely blame Simmo for that. In fact, the way I look at it, the players were more culpable. In my eight years with the team I cannot think of a player who can say, hand over heart, "Bob Simpson cost me my career." Plenty who have claimed it over a disgruntled beer cannot accept the fact that their greatest adversary was the person who is always hardest to point the finger at—the man in the mirror.

Simpson says, "I have saved more players than I burnt," which seems right to me.

Much was made of the fact that Simmo should not have been a national selector while coaching, but the argument cuts no ice with me. At best Simpson was only one of four selectors. In most senior rugby league teams or the AFL the coach is often the sole selector and therefore a more influential force than Simpson could ever have been.

Simmo was a veritable Sherlock Holmes in a green and gold track suit. He would find out in an instant if something was amiss.

From very early in my Test career I learnt not to bother trying to hide anything from him.

After my first Test match in Perth against the West Indies in 1988, at the post-Test "blowout" I severely hurt my knee doing a swallow dive rap dancing in a night club. It was not the most explainable injury, so I decided to grin and bear it, even though I was in considerable pain. But soon after the knee was acting up in a one-day match and I needed two doses of painkillers.

I had to tell Simmo, "It's not the best," which of course prompted him to ask, "How did you do it, Ian?"

I felt a bit sheepish when I explained, "Rap dancing in Perth."

"Well, it's hard to feel any sympathy for you," he said, and walked off. His body language said: totally unimpressed.

At the Nehru Cup in India in 1989 the players had a meeting about making a firm stand for better playing conditions and upgraded contracts. Secrecy was a key note of the meeting and we decided that nothing should be said to Simmo.

I think it took all of three hours for ol' glass-to-the-door Simpson to find out every solitary minute of the meeting, and six years later, when we were about to take firm action about the formation of a players association, Simmo was in on all the talks. And his imput worked well.

I didn't agree with all of Simmo's methods.

It has been said that in two of a human's five senses—sight and touch—Simpson was extremely gifted. I was told that when Simmo played Test cricket he would urge players to belt the ball harder at him at training as dumbfounded team-mates admired his freakish reflexes. That's fine if it worked for him, but it doesn't work for everybody.

The 1991 tour of the Caribbean was a tough one; Simmo seemed to be handling the Barbados leg less stressfully than either Peter Taylor or me.

If we dropped 20 hard catches in a fielding session Simmo would be quietly pleased with himself for pushing us to the limit. Simmo is credited with one of the most savage fielding sessions ever conducted—the Australian Under-19 side of 1982, when apparently he belted balls at their faces and ankles and the lads were quite shocked.

I feel that in doing this he sometimes forgot that catching is about confidence, and players need basic catches and rhythm to maintain and boost their confidence levels as well as reflexes.

When Greg Chappell practised slips catches he often caught only five or six before he walked away—in case he dropped one and lost confidence. In contrast, Simmo never seemed fully satisfied with the session unless he had extended his fieldsmen so far that they grassed a few or had taken the "spectacular" of the month.

There were times when the boys would endeavour to shorten fielding sessions by peppering Simmo with balls that landed short of where they were supposed to. But it never worked. I have seen him cop some thunderous blows on the ankles, body and head during fielding training, some from ricochets, others from direct hits, but he rarely if ever showed pain ... the most I've seen was a five second limp.

It was said that during his captaincy years, Simpson's mind was as unchangeable as the alphabet. To manufacture a Simmoism, Bob never got caught in two-man's land. But he did mellow.

After a session with Rod Marsh in a Perth park, I was convinced that rhythm and tempo catches were the way to go for a 'keeper. Sure, there is a time and place for the difficult, instinct catches, but first you have to find a groove and build your confidence.

Because Simmo was trying to wrong foot me at training my footwork wasn't developing as it should have been. I was having to dive and go the wrong and long way all the time, so I decided, after consultation with Marsh, that it was time to change.

When I explained this to Simmo, he acceded to my request. He would say, "What would you like today, Ian?" and it worked well. For a man of 60, Simpson moved with the times admirably.

Just because Simmo was the team coach didn't mean he escaped the boys' micky-taking—yours truly donning a Fred Flintstone mask at training and marching around in Simmo's typically businesslike way, bow-legged waddle and all. While we didn't exactly see him as "one of the boys" he was close enough to be open to verbal sparring.

Simmo had a habit of mixing up words, or sentences, and within the team these slips were tagged "Simmoisms". One time he told us we simply must see the movie *"Mrs Doublemire"* starring that raucous funnyman Robin Wilson—he meant *Mrs Doubtfire* with Robin Williams.

On another occasion he was sitting next to Paul Reiffel on the team bus as we passed McDonald's, the fast food outlet widely known as the "Golden Arches". As the boys sent up a throaty cheer, Simmo turned to see what the fuss was about. He winked at Reiffel and said, "You just can't beat the ol' Golden Triangles."

I have had my blues with Simpson. At a team meeting at the start of the 1991 West Indies tour the accent was unquestionably on being positive and combative against a side who'd mentally dominated Australian teams for almost a decade.

The theme of the meeting was that we would not mentally build up the West Indies as supermen and be open-minded and positive about our chances against them.

But when Simmo announced that the tour rule would be a new ball taken after 75 instead of 85 overs (remember the Windies had all the new ball firepower!) I couldn't resist a half smart. "Oh, that means I'm going to come in for the second ball ... won't that be fun," I said.

It was one of those regrettable moments when the lips are turbo charged while the brain is in a horse and buggy. No sooner had "fun" tumbled from my lips than I wished I could have sucked it all back.

Simmo exploded. "Now that's just the type of statement we don't need, Ian." Fair enough, he was right.

Simmo and I have always argued about the amount of alcohol consumed by our side. He believes we drink too much. I contend that at times we do, but it's normally at the right times. We might not have a drink for nine days, or have a couple each night, then have a big bash at the end of a Test. I have no problem with that ... in fact, I've done much to turn this kind of celebration into an art form.

Simpson might have had the reputation of being a cross between a fearsome stepfather and the grim reaper, but I often felt he was not hard enough on the boys, particularly off the field. There were times when I felt he should have encouraged more discipline. If the Brisbane Broncos or the Carlton Aussies Rules football team were on tour as much as we are, you can bet their respective coaches would take the blokes aside for stern chats much more frequently than Simmo ever did.

Though I felt he could have been harder on the team, there were times when Simpson offered general discipline warnings that were most appropriate.

Late in the 1993 Ashes tour, when the team was becoming arrogant and dismissive of autograph hunters and motel staff, Simmo said to us at a team meeting, "We expect perfection from everyone else, but do we expect it from ourselves? You can be confident without being rude and arrogant."

If you told Simpson about your problems the chances were you would be well on the way to fixing the problem before it got to the selectors. Keep it to yourself, and the chances were it would fester away without treatment and it could be months before you'd work your way back into form. I know for a fact when you confessed your problems to Simmo all he would try to do was help you. Why wouldn't he? His job was on the line too. Like him or not—many didn't—you were all in it together. The better you played, the better he looked.

Mark Taylor has an excellent up-front relationship with Simmo, but Allan Border never did. AB let Simmo run the show when he had the leadership thrust upon him; because Simmo had his hands on the wheel for so long, AB couldn't suddenly say, "Well, hang on Bob, you sit down. I'll take it from here," once the hard years had been swept away by a new era of prosperity.

He never thought he could do it, so AB never got to that level of communication with him. When Taylor was made captain of Australia and myself his deputy, one of our goals was to work closely with Simmo so that we could get the most out of him and, consequently, the team.

Simmo is not a great one for sympathy, but he is acutely aware of what type of help players need at different times.

On my first tour, Pakistan, I became ill on the rest day of the First Test and told him I'd been struck down with stomach and bowel problems. Reading

*Simmo and AB. It was a partnership that pulled Australia
out of a deep hole through the '80s.*

the situation well, he told me my problem was just nerves and would pass in a day, then walked off immediately. I was of course doing it tough, looking for the sympathy vote and, quite rightly, he wasn't going to give it to me. Yes, my problem was just nerves and yes, it did pass in a day.

Rather than be sympathetic, he would normally have a working suggestion. Instead of saying, "Bad luck about today," he'd offer advice on how to fix it tomorrow. It's his way, and I think it's the best. We are playing such a tough form of sport, there is no place for mollycoddling.

HE SAYS, SHE SAYS

*"If you want to have a long-lasting cricket career
you must have a supportive wife or be single.
Anything in between and you couldn't do it."*

ALLAN BORDER

So how does a marriage survive the pressures of a seemingly endless summer of long absences from home?

When I first started in the Australian team I never liked the wives being around. The team was everything to me and I just wanted to concentrate on cricket.

It took me a long time to adjust when I got home. The most stressful time of the summer for me was at Christmas when the wives came to the Melbourne Test match. It was foreign to me to have some-one else to consider when I was playing cricket.

It is amazing to watch the way some players change around their wives. In my life I've always tried to be consistent no matter what company I'm in. Helen foots the bill for this because she puts up with some rubbish at times, but I don't want to be Dr Jeckyll with her and Mr Hyde with the team. Sometimes I see a player in the presence of his wife and think, "Is this the man I knew a week ago?"

Helen is excellent at Christmas time, for she knows the demands of the cricket are quite excessive, and I will always appreciate the major sacrifices she makes. I can recall the time she took Emma down to the motel foyer at 4am when we had a Test that morning and Emma could not settle.

My priorities have changed as time has passed. During the 1989 Ashes tour I made an entry in my diary that said, "Remember ... family is the most important thing to me." I wouldn't make that entry now, because I don't have to remind myself that family is number one. I can switch from concentrating on cricket to concentrating on family very easily. In my early years I knew deep down that cricket wasn't the most important thing in my life, but if I hadn't made it a top priority I would never have been a successful player.

These days I wouldn't mind having Helen and the kids on every tour because I know I could handle it. But I can see the drawbacks. When the Australian team is on tour without the wives we tend to go out in big groups and often meet in the motel bar after the game for an unofficial team bonding session. When the wives are there the group is splintered. The single guys tend to knock around together and the married players ponder where they will take the girls that night.

Unlike the players, who are there for the cricket, the wives tend to want to do the tourist thing, so that creates further pressure. The team focus isn't as great as it should be.

I feel the way we operate at the moment, where the players concentrate on their cricket at the start of the tour and then are joined by their wives near the end, is the perfect compromise.

The more I mix with old cricketers the more I am convinced that the lot of the cricketer hasn't changed much over the years. The wives-on-tour issue is an old chestnut. Wives were banned from major Australian tours from 1921 until after World War II, prompting the clever headline in war-torn England, "Australia Rules the Wives".

Motel life can really soften the domestic skills of the over-pampered cricketer. I am a hopeless cook and, until recently, I thought a wok was something you threw at a wabbit.

It is quite common for a cricketer to come home from tour, sit down to a meal and then say to his wife, "Where's the sauce?" and quite rightly receive the reply of, "You've got two legs ... it's in the cupboard." Jane Border used to give Allan the infamous empty stubby test to monitor his awareness of household chores. AB would leave an empty stubby beside his lounge chair and Jane would deliberately leave it to see how long it would be before he'd pick it up. I think four days was about the longest.

Border's best mate Pat Welsh tells the story of having AB around for dinner when Jane was in hospital giving birth to their third child Tara. He said AB was so exhausted at minding the kids for a couple of days that he slumped in the lounge chair sound asleep by 8pm. He was a total wreck. When he asked AB how cooking for the kids was going, he said, "Not too bad. We had Pizza Hut last night, McDonald's the night before and we're planning to go to Hungry Jack's tomorrow."

Just because you can score more than 10 000 Test runs doesn't mean you can cook spaghetti.

Children inevitably become much more attached to Mum than Dad. I remember playing with Laura in the back yard and she hurt her foot. I tried to pick her up but that made her howl and she ran straight to Helen. We can be playing together and everything is fine, but when trouble intervenes I disappear in her eyes and she only wants Mum.

Being away from daughter Emma is one of the challenging aspects of touring life.

Phone calls with Emma can be quite interesting. I once asked her whether she missed me. "No Daddy, but I love you," was her quaint reply. Sometimes I send postcards to Emma that are effectively to Helen. When Emma was eight months I sent one saying, "Dear Emma, How are you going? If Mum doesn't burp, bath or feed you properly, just bite her boob off ..."

Emma was born when I was in the West Indies on the 1991 tour and my first sighting of her was via a fax sent by *The Courier-Mail* in Brisbane, who had sent a photographer to the hospital.

I was rooming with Merv Hughes at the time, and was about to go out with the boys when he said, "By the way, Helen rang and she's having contractions." Helen and I had been waiting for the birth of our first child but I was well schooled in Merv's tomfoolery and I wasn't going to fall for his flimsy prank. Merv insisted he was serious and kept at me the next morning, while I just laughed him off.

Finally, I decided to call home just on the off chance he was serious. Helen confirmed Merv was telling the truth, and I cringed with embarrassment.

Border's quote at the start of this chapter is totally true. To be at the top for a long period you must have a supportive wife, or be single. Helen knows me so well she can bring me back into gear by a simple statement. In an understated way, she can often read me better than I read myself and will chime in with just the right line, like, "You are worrying too much."

I'll never forget the day I met her. It was a humid January morn in 1981 and I was practising with the Brisbane State High School first XI a week before school started. I had just moved down from Biloela and had been placed in the main cricket squad to train for the new summer.

During a break in training the boys were sitting around in the deserted school grounds and a group of new Year 8 students were led past us by a shapely Year 12 student, their chaperone for the day. Our admiring glances trailed her as one, much like those tennis crowds you see following the path of a ball in a rally. I was most impressed. In fact I was so impressed I decided to marry her ... but not for another seven years.

There were several qualities I found most attractive about her. She had a touch of innocence that made people think she was a nice person, but complementing this were confidence and personality.

During my last year at school I got to know Helen through mutual friends. Our first date was no Romeo and Juliet affair ... I simply escorted her to a hockey match she was playing in. As is always the case with school romances, our relationship involved small dashes of improvisation and brinkmanship ... or should I say brinkwomanship?

Helen's parents gave her a strict 10pm curfew, and if we went to the pictures she would have to be on the steps of the theatre right at that time so her mother could pick her up. Often, we would sneak off to the now abolished New York Hotel instead, and join our school mates for some beers before rushing Helen back to the theatre steps by 10.

I am not sure how I wooed Helen, but it certainly wasn't by overwhelming her with material wealth. Most of our early dates were in my trusty vehicle, a yellow Cortina called Christina. Our relationship sustained an early test when we left school and she went off to train as a nurse in Gympie, a few hours drive north of Brisbane, while I stayed on for teacher's college. During her three years in Gympie she often drove down to Brisbane as we stoked the embers of a challenging, yet workable long-distance relationship.

Within a few years we both felt ready to tie the knot, and I became a privileged member of the Perkins family, and she of mine.

A favourite story that confirms my status as the royal son-in-law dates back to Christmas day in the mid-'80s.

I have always enjoyed Christmas, especially in those years, with family around and no pressures of a Test match the next day. The sound of Dad cracking the first beer of the day was music to my ears. It was the starting gun for an afternoon of solid drinking.

On this particular day we had Christmas dinner at my family's place, then headed over to the Perkins' for supper. As tends to be the case when I've had a few beers, I was bristling with cheek when I arrived and proceeded to take the mickey out of the inlaws in a light-hearted sort of way.

Full of booze, I dived in the pool and cut my arm on the bottom as I was swimming around.

There was blood everywhere and within seconds I resembled a fallen war hero who'd staggered home for treatment as the Perkins family swarmed around me with lavish attention. Don Perkins even cooked me up a batch of my favourite pancakes with eggs, bacon and syrup.

Everyone seemed concerned except my disbelieving brother-in-law Ian, who stood, stubby in hand, shaking his head. He said, "How about this bloke ... He's arrived here full of booze, taken the piss out of everyone, left blood in the pool and now gets first class medical attention and his favourite meal ... unbelievable."

I ring home about twice a week when on tour. And Helen rings me more than I ring her, because international hotels normally charge an exhorbitant fee for phone calls.

Players have different habits. Craig McDermott is a great one for making many calls home—sometimes four a day—even if they are only short calls. Michael Slater doesn't mind a lengthy chat on the phone home, but the phone bill champion is Glenn 'Pigeon' McGrath, who spends more time in phone booths than Superman. Glenn gets so attached to his girlfriends he occasionally rings them twice a day at an hour a time. Goodness knows what they talk about. Surely not his new pig-shooting magazines.

FROM THE BETTER HALF

"It's funny to read Ian's description of his first sighting of me, because I can remember seeing him only a week later walking to the library and thinking, "I wouldn't mind marrying him." It was an unusual thought, considering we had only spoken a few times to each other and weren't even going out. But we have always had a good rapport and we read each other very well.

Being the wife of a professional cricketer is a case of sinking or swimming. It is a hard lifestyle, though there are also rewards. Some women can cope okay, but others find they need support or it is simply not their cup of tea.

The fact that we have had distance in our relationship from the time I was nursing in Gympie helped me and Ian cope when the distance became greater in later years. I do miss having him around, but I try not to dwell on it.

When he comes home there is an adjustment period for all of us—he has to get used to family life and the family has to get used to the individuality Ian builds up over months of having only himself to care for and everything done for him.

When I look back now at Ian's years in the Australian team, I do feel a little envious of the great worldly experiences he's had, but the scales are balanced now because, as much as he still loves the fast-moving lifestyle, he

SUN NEWSPAPERS LIBRARY

Helen cradles a newly born Emma who is clutching a photo of her absent father.

concedes he is missing out on something special by not being at home with the kids.

When Ian comes home after a tour the kids swoon after him and I become a fly on the wall for a couple of weeks.

Jane Border has become a role model for me, because I admired the way she carried herself with confidence and got on with her life without Allan. She is very selfless. She's not a lady who spends a lot of time in the media, but whatever she says makes good sense."

HELEN HEALY

THE BOYS

*"The only thing I'll say to you tonight is to enjoy your
years in the side, because when you look back you will remember
them as the best of your life."*

ROD MARSH DURING AN ADDRESS TO THE AUSTRALIAN CRICKET SIDE

It has been said that the Australian cricket team is a bit like a family, though at times we are much closer than that.

Families might see each other in the morning for breakfast and at night for dinner, but how many of them spend all day together, working, playing, training, dining, celebrating, commiserating and travelling.

Very few I would think.

You get to know all about each other very quickly, so I felt it was appropriate we spotlight the men who have been such a big part of my life over the past few years.

MARK TAYLOR

'Tubsy' has a good sense of humour and the ability to cop a sledge and a joke and return serve before the first barb has crossed the net. He gives more than he cops and does not hold back in taking the mickey out of team-mates. When he jabs at you there is a veritable barrel full of comebacks. Your options are as wide as Tubby's well-nourished thighs.

We tend to counter him by targeting his jughead or his backside—I understand he wears the same size underpants as Pavarotti.

Speaking of clothes swapping, there has always been a suspicion that Tubby could well be Bob Simpson's love child. The rumours started on a Gold Coast golf course several years ago when Tubby and Simmo were walking off the ninth green towards the clubhouse.

You should have seen it. They had the same white floppy hat on and, with their identically sized legs and backsides, were walking stride for stride beside each other with a rhythm that would be the envy of any synchronised swimming pair.

They were cricket's version of the swivelite guys. I was playing in the group behind them and someone said, "Have a go at those two—which one is Tubby?"

The captain and his deputy have always had a good working relationship.

Tubby has the reputation for being a poor dresser and it is well-founded. If we are in a shop looking at clothes and we all agree there is one obscene shirt we don't like, it's a sure bet Tubby will like it.

But he is so strong-willed he will stick to his opinion and buy it and wear it regularly.

Mark did not stumble into the position of Australian captain. He prepared himself meticulously for the role.

In his last year as vice-captain he took a step back from some of the players he had grown from boys to men with, and prepared himself for the major role shift from one of the boys to national captain.

Yet a substantial part of him will remain one of the boys.

When Tubby and Michael Slater batted quite slowly on the fourth day of play in the First Test against New Zealand at the WACA in the 1993–94 summer, an impatient Perth crowd started a chant demanding more urgency.

Tubbs was furious when he came back to the room, and as he ripped off his pads said, "Bloody WACA crowds." Steve Waugh, who obviously felt the crowd had a point, quipped "Actually mate, that was us ... we started the chant."

It proved that being captain didn't mean he was above the occasional prod from the boys.

Tubbsy has no problem disciplining his side or sharply pulling them into line. Glenn McGrath and Matt Hayden discovered this when he dressed them down after they had an on-field stoush during an Australia–Australia-A clash in Sydney several years ago.

In this regard he differs in style from Allan Border, who didn't like to confront blokes. Tubbsy has no problems with it and makes sure the team is running the way he wants it to run. He doesn't simply lead by example as AB liked to. Communication is the biggest feature of Taylor's leadership. He is a meticulous planner and that is another strength of his captaincy.

But no matter how many hours' forethought he puts into a game, he will react quickly and instinctively and toss Plan A in the dust bin if it doesn't work.

MICHAEL SLATER

There is an ancient theory which I have always subscribed to that people play their sport in the same manner they live their life. The very embodiment of this theory is Michael Slater.

Slats lives life as he bats ... at breakneck speed.

He drives fast and he loves fast cars. Before I went skiing with him for the first time in the winter of 1995 I would have bet anything he would be the original Kamikaze man down the slopes.

Sure enough, with no technique, he would go flat out until he had a spill, then he would get up, shake himself off, and scoot off again.

Being an all-action person, Slats hates sitting around.

My favourite Slats story concerned the night in Melbourne when he slept-walked in the nude outside his motel room and couldn't get back in because the door closed behind him.

He had to retreat to a fire exit, where he had an anxious and extended stay before discovering an empty black garbage bag several flights below.

He gained some measure of self-respect by pushing his legs through the bottom of the bag to cover himself. Looking as though he had just fallen off a float at the Sydney Mardi Gras, he managed to rouse motel security, who escorted him back to his room with no further loss of dignity.

We all have deep pride in playing for our country, but pride oozes from every pore when Slats bats for Australia.

It is this very emotion that makes him drive himself relentlessly in fitness workouts. He is a strong little bloke and is desperate to do anything that will help him in a game situation.

For all the bristling bravado Slats displays in opening the batting, off the field he has a soft side which can make him vulnerable to the occasional psychological bruise.

Some players, when receiving a highly critical letter that is part of life at the game's highest level, will toss it in the bin and never give it so much as a passing thought.

But Slats is such a softie when it comes to things like this and gets deeply offended.

Bad press also offends and worries him.

Slats is also a real socialite.

When he goes to guest speaking nights, it is the devil's own job to drag him away from tables. Because he is so naturally chatty and polite, he wants to stay until every query is answered and autograph signed. He puts a lot of energy into people. Around Australia there would be thousands of people from Perth to Penrith who would have told relatives what a nice fellow Slats is.

DAVID BOON

Australian cricket made a hard-living legend of Boonie in the same way it did Doug Walters a decade ago—and personally, I am not sure either man deserved the title.

To hear all the stories built into the Walters legend, you would swear he spent half of his life with a beer in hand captivating a bar room audience with rowdy tales of yesteryear.

I haven't found him like that at all. He does sit at the bar, but he is a fairly reserved character who tells the odd dry yarn in a nice quiet way.

Boonie is much the same. He is a strong man and a tough individual to get on top of. I rate this quality in cricketers because it is the one trait which I have tried to hone in my own game.

Boonie's great sporting hero was Carlton's long-haired legend Bruce 'The Flying Doormat' Doull, whom Boonie admired "because of the efficient but low-key way he went about his job".

Many admire Boon for the same reason.

He was a heavy duty Test batsman who liked to tune his walkman to heavy metal music when he wasn't instigating wrestling matches on the team bus. These were among his favourite past-times and he was always hard to beat, because he had the strength of the Budda he always looked like at the crease.

His method of batting success became a simple matter of playing well within his limitations, forcing bowlers to think that they were going to have to do something different or special to get him out.

This often prompted them to produce a speculative or wayward ball that he'd efficiently pick off.

ALLAN BORDER

Of all the admirable qualities of Allan Border, the one I mention most often to people is what an unchangeable character he remained throughout the game's most enduring Test career.

From the moment I met him a decade ago to the day he retired from cricket in Melbourne at the end of the 1995–96 summer, he never changed a bit.

I like him so much because there is no sham about him. He is who he is.

In some ways this has been to his detriment. In the early 1980s he might have told a cameraman to "get that camera out of my face" if he overstepped the mark. A decade later, even with the responsibility of the captaincy, he would do the same, without being fully aware of or caring about the fuss it would create.

I admired his fearless will in these situations, but I also learnt that you have to handle the media with care, because its misrepresentations can tarnish people's perceptions of you if allowed to continue.

The stress of being Australia's brightest star and its beast of burden for all those years was only apparent very late in his career, when he started to get asthma in the dressing room as he waited to bat. There's no doubt that as AB's career reached its twilight years he became anxious to live up to expectations. Occasionally in a Shield game, or a touring match or even a dead Test, he would drop down the order and send me in front of him. He just didn't really want to bat, to put it all on the line just for the sake of it.

He was the best "bad day" batsman in the game. Even when he was in the most dire of form troughs, when his bat might have felt the width of a carrot, he could still fashion a fiesty 50.

Where eagles dare. The boys summon up the courage to take a flight in an Army helicopter during the tour to South Africa in 1994.

For AB it was always a matter of how many rather than how. He was a team man till the end.

Bowlers lifted 10 per cent when he came to the crease. West Indian Malcolm Marshall loved bowling at AB and went into an uncontrollable victory dance whenever he got him out.

His presence also lifted bowlers on his side. Queensland left-armer Dirk Tazelaar, speaking at his own Testimonial dinner, said he'd often looked up when about to bowl at AB standing at slip and thought how important it was that he bowled well in front of such a great player.

Border was a selfless character who always put the team first. In England in 1989 he could have earnt the equivalent of a yearly wage for a few simple hours work by signing up as a newspaper columnist for one of the tabloid papers.

He knew that if he signed up with *The Mirror*, that paper's arch tabloid rival, *The Sun*, would make him a target and try to soil his image and that could destabilise the team.

So he simply wasn't interested. It was yet another example of the selfless things Border did for the team but got no credit for.

He hated to impose himself on anyone, to tinker with their thought processes on the game. People felt because of his grand depth of knowledge and experience he should have been advising players and shaping their thinking.

I do not believe AB was a natural leader—particularly off the field—and that meant he had to put more pressure on himself to do it well.

Certainly by the time I played with him he was a fine on-field general, but I don't think he ever felt totally at peace with the demands of the media and the administration. He steered away from that and was basically a cricket captain.

His only downside as a captain is that he didn't think he had to motivate blokes. He thought if they could not motivate themselves they should not be playing for Australia.

I don't quite buy this theory—not with the massive amount of cricket we play. I think all players occasionally need some-one to pep them up.

Invariably when AB let fly at a team-mate it was because they had showed him a lack of respect, as I did during the Cape Town Test against South Africa in 1993–94.

Chasing 361 we were 3–153 before Border consolidated the innings on the third day, but he was struggling desperately for runs between lunch and tea that day.

Like New Zealand's John Wright, AB would tend to get frustrated and angry at himself when he wasn't batting as well as he could have.

I compounded his anguish with a poorly timed practical joke when I picked up his bat after he entered the rooms at tea and went to place it in an ice

Left: *Recognise the "that's for you" bat point? It's me, doing my Dean Jones impression.*

Below: *My Tim May impression.*

PETER CRONIN

PETER CRONIN

bucket, as if to say "Hey, we better cool this baby down, it's running too hot."

AB, feeling I was mocking his best efforts, was not impressed. He snapped at me with the words "Listen mate, I am batting my arse off out there ... why don't you go and play with your schoolboy mates."

Border's popularity in Queensland is evident from an anecdote from the Bulls month celebrations after the Sheffield Shield final win of 1994–95.

Because of television commitments in the Caribbean, Border could not attend the side's country tour where the Shield was taken by the players to townships from Cairns to Longreach.

But at each venue the players took a cardboard cutout of AB which they raised as he was introduced to the crowd. AB always got the loudest cheer, even though he wasn't there.

MICHAEL BEVAN

A very introverted person who is aware of this trait and is teaching himself to come out of his shell.

People see his batting, with its wide range of strokes and quick-stepping brilliance, and think it spawns exclusively from natural brilliance. In fact it is governed by a very calculating brain.

He is such a good thinker on batting in one-day cricket that in the World Cup he was asked to address the side on how to bat in the last 10 overs.

He is aware of the nature of his technique and when to play what stroke. He specifies a couple of areas of the field which he targets for fours and if he can't hit a four he will hit a single.

In his younger days he was known for his displays of temper, known as "Bev Attacks", and he has been known to have a shower with his gear still on and bash the occasional locker.

But he has worked hard on mellowing his temperament.

Where a few of the boys might carry a Penthouse magazine in their kit bags, he will carry a muscle mag, for he is a committed gym man.

STEVE WAUGH

The Waugh twins, Steve and Mark, were so engrossed in sport as youngsters they had quite a naive upbringing.

It is legend that well into their late teens the boys played any type of sport until dusk provided a fulltime hooter. If they had had any more ball skills they would have bounced.

They could do everything except swim. Quite amazingly given their prowess at most other sports, I am told Steve and Mark sunk like human starfish whenever they entered the water during school carnivals.

They were the real Aussie outdoor boys but this left relatively little time for the normal teenage distractions of partying and alcohol.

Even now Steve admits he hears tales of other players in their hell-raising youth and thinks, "I wasn't doing that when I was 17."

In his early years, struggling to bridge the gap between potential and performance, he became quite introverted and short with people.

These days he puts a lot of time into others and the young blokes tend to gravitate towards him.

Players like Justin Langer, Greg Blewett and Shane Warne have all used him as a confidante and been better players for it.

The Waugh brothers were born to be sportsmen rather than students - though Steve deserves credit for his ingenuity in at least one school exam.

He was asked to measure the circumference of a circle which was printed to scale on the examination paper. Instead of getting bogged down by arithmetic, he plucked out a hair, curled it around the circle, measured it and whacked in the answer.

How Steve packs his suit case and gear coffin is beyond all of us. So much gear bobbles out of his coffin during a match that it always appears he will need another one. Yet he simply jumps up and down on it until it closes.

Steve's interest in the game's history is as genuine as that of the most obsessed cricket fan. For years he has been chasing a signed photo of the 1948 Australian side and has memorabilia hunters throughout the world on alert to snaffle one for him as soon as they see it.

The keenest bower bird in our team, he has hundreds of old shirts and pants stocked in his Sydney home along with a bail signed by Sir Donald Bradman, the last pair of boots Allan Border wore in Test cricket, Geoff Lawson's last pair of Test boots, a stump from Australia's 1987 World Cup win, and more than 1500 photos.

Steve's love for the game is evident as much by his attitude to club cricket as to Test matches. He always puts his hand up for grade cricket for his beloved Bankstown and rues the fact he cannot play there more often.

Though top grade players can earn high four figure sums in Sydney, Steve said it would be as waste of time approaching him because he is a Bankstown boy and that's the end of the matter.

MARK WAUGH

In a casino in Sri Lanka several years ago Mark Waugh was walking away from a table when he picked up his last chip of the night and tossed it nonchalantly over his left shoulder onto the roulette table like a rugby league player hurling a speculator pass.

With all eyes upon it, the chip did a rolling lap of the board, settled on number 16 and the crowd at the table erupted as the number came up just as Mark was shuffling off.

Welcome to the world of Australians cricket's Flash Harry ... our Mr Natural.

Mark has natural flamboyance in most areas of his life. As a punter he

*Some golf course hazards are more hazardous than others; at the 13th
at the Lost City course in Sun City, South Africa, wayward hook shots end
up in the crocodile pit.*

will have as much on a 50-1 pop as he will on a favourite because, as he says,
"A horse doesn't know what price it is."

A few years ago when Michael Whitney brought a didgeridoo into the New
South Wales dressing room he asked the boys to have a try. Several of them
couldn't blow a note.

Mark Waugh, who had never tackled one before, blew it so well if you
had tossed a beard on him people would have thought he was a young Rolf
Harris.

He makes things look easy. When he started to take off-spinning seriously
at the start of the 1995-96 summer it took him a New York minute to work
out the ideal off-spinner's field. Some spinners take seasons to get it right.

He is often coming up with useful data for our game plans. When I mentioned that he would have made a good first class captain to some journalists in Bombay during the last World Cup, Mark was standing behind me
and overheard the conversation.

When asked by the journalists how he felt about captaincy, he said some
thing like, "I felt I could have handled it and would have really enjoyed it.
But the circumstances never really came up where I had the chance to do it."

He is the original pretty boy who is always fiddling with his hair, particularly when he takes his fielding hat off. How he hates having ruffled hair,
for heaven's sake.

The relationship between the Waugh brothers is an occasional source of
amusement to the team.

They have a rule that they never touch each other in photos. News Limited's Ray Titus made it a personal goal on the last West Indian tour to get a photo of the Waugh brothers touching and it took an Australian Frank Worrell Trophy win to get it.

Finally, in the glorious euphoria, the boys relented and put their arms around each other as they cradled the trophy.

I think the brotherly embrace, which oozed immense natural warmth, lasted all of point five of a second before the boys shot off to separate corners of the dressing room muttering something about "being made to look like dags".

CRAIG McDERMOTT

I can speak with some authority on Craig McDermott, because I first saw him bowl at primary school level when I was a 12-year-old domiciled at Biloela and he was an 11-year-old Ipswich star.

He has always been an exceptional player. In recent years he has been the one Australian fast bowler who consistently knows where each ball is going.

He has great control, knows a lot about bowling, has the confidence to try, and get away with, experimental balls because he practices them so often.

His ability to keep pressure on batsmen has peaked since 1988, when he took on a spartan fitness regime that gave him the confidence to bowl for much longer than other bowlers.

He could bowl 10 or 11 overs at full pace and batsmen just wouldn't get a let-up.

I know Billy so well I can tell by his body language how he is likely to bowl on any given day. I would like to see him bluff the opposition more on days when he is not feeling great.

The other truly great fast bowlers, with Dennis Lillee the standout, looked the same every hostile day of their working life. No doubt underneath there were times when they felt they were running on one cylinder powered by two-stroke fuel. But you never knew.

Craig is the most meticulous, mess-free character I have met. Mr Sheen is a disorganised grub compared to Billy.

You could eat your dinner out of his coffin in the dressing room ... but don't dare leave a gravy stain.

He lines his sweat bands up beside each other and his socks are neatly folded ... all 50 pairs of them.

Of the many quick spells he has bowled I understand the fastest was a hurricane down-wind effort with a roaring gale at his back against Tasmania in Launceston in 1984–85, just before he gained Test selection.

He broke Tasmanian skipper Brian Davidson's arm taking 6-45, and bowled so swiftly that Rob Kerr, standing at the gully, was closer to the boundary than the batsman.

GLENN McGRATH

The man they call 'Pigeon' has different tastes to a lot of us.

He will carry a "How to kill and skin a pig" video on tour, but I don't know that he has ever watched it.

In South Africa he was proudly displaying the duty free tripod he bought for a camera. Everyone was waiting for him to show off the camera to go with it—but it never appeared and still hasn't, two years later.

He likes guns and combat and is always thinking about how he would knock a bloke out, yet to look at him you'd swear he wouldn't tackle a ham sandwich. In fact, I don't think he's ever been in a fight.

Yet he is a bloke who will have a dirty big go for you—nothing much scares him—and he is good value for the team for he's a bit like Merv Hughes with his on-field clout and off-field playfulness.

McGrath is a very fit bowler. He is quite strong and the biomechanics of his sound action are such that he should not be struck down with many injuries. Mike Whitney said at the start of McGrath's Test career that he was "Curtly Ambrose thin rather than Bruce Reid thin", meaning that McGrath's frame, while sinewy, was far from frail.

His modest batting efforts are a welcome source of amusement to the team.

I have never a seen a player edge the first ball so often when he bats in the nets. Steve Waugh has a theory that Glenn is actually left-handed.

His signature shot is not the hook or the cut, but the one that bowls him off his left foot when it makes contact half a metre outside leg-stump and comes back onto the stumps. No-one else ever seems to get out that way - yet it's happened to him four times.

There have been occasions when he has been so frustrated with his batting it has threatened to affect his bowling. I remember once after he scored a duck in a one-day match at the Adelaide Oval he was simply devastated.

He smashed his coffin, wouldn't eat his lunch and spent the entire lunch break sulking. We felt he was on the verge of retirement and it affected him so deeply he could barely be bothered concentrating on his bowling when he took the field.

He went on to take four wickets in an innings and win a man-of-the-match award. It was an unbelievable transformation.

In our Brisbane training camp the week before the World Cup, McGrath was involved in a comical incident in the nets. He actually struck one in the middle and hooked a high full toss out of the nets and towards the local police station.

It was a recurring problem for Simmo that our practice balls keep disappearing, and no sooner had Glenn hit the stroke than Simmo erupted with "Right Glenn, if you are going to bat like that we'll call off the session ... get out here."

TIM MAY

Tim is a conservative character by nature but I feel that time and the experience of being thrust into different environments has made him a more outward person.

Yet despite this he hates the spotlight which, of course, makes him a direct contrast to his long-time spinning partner, the great showman Warne.

He used to work as an accountant at the Commonwealth Bank and I can just imagine him wearing the grey cardigan, grey slip-on shoes, and beige bell-bottom slacks each day of his working life. These qualities made him captain of 'our nerds'.

But now that he's left the Bank and become more experienced in the business world as the proprietor of two successful night spots in Adelaide, his whole demeanour has changed for the better.

He used to be cynical and self-contained, but now his cynicism is reflected mainly in his whipcord sense of humour.

His batting has blossomed exceptionally since his 42 not out against the West Indies at Adelaide in 1993, for he has tightened his technique and learnt to bat without taking risks ... to bat for other players.

His best bowling for Australia came on the 1993 Ashes tour when he was gaining tantalising drift away from the batsmen and sharp spin back.

PAUL REIFFEL

Known as 'The Wingman', he is one of those characters who is always where the action is but never at the centre of attention. He enjoys hovering quietly on the periphery.

Reiffel is an honest bloke whose success over the past few years has been due to an increase in pace. When he bowled with good control at medium pace, batsmen were able to hit him on good wickets once they were set, because they could hit through the line knowing every ball was going to be of a similar length.

But at his current rating of fast medium, the same batsmen have less time for decision-making. His batting also gives the side a lot of confidence, being a world record holder in limited-overs cricket!

ERROL ALCOTT (Physiotherapist)

'Hooter'Alcott's travelling surgery is open 24 hours, such are the demands of the job.

He has spent many a long night treating me, and as a physio he is second to none. Because he has little interest in cricket as a sport, he is very good at levelling out players' emotions after victory or defeat. He is not the sort of person who gets carried away.

He is a vital cog in the team machine and excellent at assessing the players' moods, attitudes and body conditions.

ALL IN
THE MIND

"Strength is a matter of the made-up mind."

JOHN BEECHER

A year or so after the start of my international career I was browsing in a book shop in Brisbane's City Plaza shopping centre when I looked up to find some long-lasting inspiration for my cricket career.

There before me was a framed copy of an unsigned poem, every word of which is, in my view, a pearl.

The poem is of unknown origins and my persistent attempts to locate its author have been fruitless, though I know it was used by American football coaches for motivation as far back as the 1950s.

I have titled the poem "Winning".

> *If you think you are beaten you are*
> *If you think you are not you don't*
> *If you would like to win but think you can't*
> *You almost certainly won't.*
> *If you think you'll lose — you've lost*
> *For out in the world you'll find*
> *Success begins with a fellow's will*
> *It's all in the state of mind.*
> *For many a race is lost*
> *Before a step is run*
> *And many a coward fails*
> *Before his work has begun.*
> *Think big and your deeds will grow*
> *Think small and you'll fall behind*
> *Think that you can and you will*
> *It's all in the state of mind.*
> *Life's battles don't always go*
> *To the stronger or faster man*
> *But sooner or later the man who wins*
> *Is the fellow who thinks he can.*

I love this poem because it brings your thoughts back to the right way of thinking. It is relevant not only to cricket, but any sport, and life.

You can mould your whole thinking around it and I consider Steve Waugh is the very personification of it.

Every year I keep a performance diary which contains a daily assessment of my form throughout the summer, and my first task when I start a new diary is to write my favourite poem in the front it. I read the words at least once a month.

If Steve Waugh told me he had this bat on a piece of string I'd be inclined to believe him.

187

Keeping a diary is important to me. Why? To explain this I defer to a favourite Forrest Gump quote which is in one of my diaries. It says, "You can never fully move on to your future until you have dealt with your past."

These are my feelings precisely. I am a paper person. If I don't write things down they muddle around in my head and I don't deal with them as quickly, or effectively. By writing my thoughts down I can literally close the book on that day's play and move on to tomorrow knowing my performance has been scrutinised and categorised.

The diaries are essential to me. When I was studying to be a teacher we covered sports psychology and it taught me that the world's premier athletes kept intricate diaries of their performance and preparation. Cricketers generally don't but in so many ways cricket is 10–15 years behind other sports, not as professional as it could be.

My diaries help me solve problems which might recur. They show I have the same problems at similar stages of most seasons. Without the diary, the problem might linger undetected for two weeks then require another two weeks to remedy. That represents a month of below par form and resultant pressure build-up from the fans and media.

So, when I'm looking for a remedy, I can look back at last year's diary to find out what led to it, what went wrong and how I fixed it.

An example is coping with tiredness. Sometimes cricketers don't even know when they are tired, but through my diaries I have formed small check points which alert me. If I am getting irritable with people, particularly autograph hunters, I know it is a sign I am drifting off the pace. I will note this and take corrective action, perhaps lighten off training for a week or maybe train even harder depending on the circumtances and stage of the season.

People have said to me that I am mentally tough. I am not super tough, but I am mentally aware of what goes on in my game, what could happen to my game and how to fix it.

When I first started at Test level I could never recover from a bad start to the day. Now I use skills and thought processes to get my game and my mind back on track.

The diaries are more than just a cold assessment of performance. They also revive memories of team-mates, and other magic moments.

Merv Hughes, with his penchant for always being in the frontline of dressing room mayhem, figures more prominently in the diaries than any other player—22 entries!

These range from the day he drank the entire cocktail list after an Ashes Test win in 1989 to the time in Barbados when he threw his sweaty, tacky old bowling shoes out the window to dry, then later, when he walked into the nearby casino, saw them gracing the feet of an old local sailor.

Then there was the time I was batting with Allan Border in Christchurch

FROM THE HEALY DIARIES

"I want to be the best 'keeper in the world. Tomorrow is a good place to start."—6 OCTOBER 1990

"My integrity was questioned again when Hooper was bowled. I've got very serious about what's happening. I am near retirement. Must sort the situation out. Can't let it worry me but accept that people are now split in their opinion of me, and get on with things. A 'keeper's lot is in amongst it and I can't back away from it. I must lighten up about it and accept it as part of my job and contribute to a team victory no matter what. I now dislike the opposition."—MY EMOTIONS REACH FLASHPOINT IN THE AFTERMATH OF THE BRIAN LARA STUMPING INCIDENT IN THE 1991–92 SEASON

"So depressed about my batting and general persona ... negative, internal and quiet. I have never had a history of being scared of being dropped. This has reduced my intensity and performance. So what. I failed with the bat. Get on with it and keep throwing punches. Don't take the easy option of giving it all up."—MORE ANGUISH AFTER THE LARA INCIDENT AND BEING BOOED IN PERTH.

"If you eliminate the fear of death you can become invincible."
—THE MOVIE *BODYGUARD* FEBRUARY 1992

"No practice Friday, drunk Thursday. No diary write up, no goals to over-ride negative thoughts. Consequently felt more nervous and focus on the ball was down. Wasted an opportunity to continue my quest to be the best 'keeper. Not a good sign for a professional."—OCTOBER 1990

"It's not what lies ahead which holds us back but what has gone before. Don't worry about what has gone before."—JANUARY 1990

"Think about it. Love your job. Bat like a batsman and not like a tailender. Too many things flood the mind. Have fun. Stay there. Withdraw from the atmosphere and distractions."—20 SEPTEMBER 1990

"Champions and cowards are exactly the same inside. Scared of dying. It's what one does that makes him a champ and what one doesn't do that makes him a coward."

"You pay the price of success in advance, you pay the price of failure forever."—GREG CHAPPELL

"Inconvenience is temporary ... rewards are permanent."
—GREG CHAPPELL, AGAIN

"Missed just three chances this season, two diving chances off Bruce Reid in Melbourne and a stumping in Brisbane. So good statistically. My 'keeping to the quicks was exceptional in all forms of the game. My body position was good ... low, flexed and balanced which allowed me to move powerfully in a low sideways motion. Diving catches were possible due to this good starting position."—FROM THE WRAP-UP OF MY 1991-92 SEASON

"To win without risk is to triumph without glory."—JANUARY 1992

FROM THE HEALY DIARIES

"When we are down, myself included, I must be the determined, positive and encouraging person. My performance will rub off on the team."—STILL FINDING MY FEET IN TEST CRICKET IN NOVEMBER 1988

"We are all afraid of something. It tells us and lets us know we care for things and don't wish to lose them."—UNKNOWN SOURCE, FEBRUARY 1992

"The most gutless shot I have played in my career. I deserved to be dropped for lack of pride. Attempted swish across the line against the spin. Straight up in the air caught by Prabhakar off Shastri. One session to bat, five down ... nice time to have brain fade you weak (expletive deleted). Whole match terrible team performance."—3 JANUARY 1992

"Compulsive hooking is basic laziness and comes through not concentrating on watching the ball and carelessly playing a shot that isn't on. Watch ball and get into position accordingly. Be strong. I have to look to play elsewhere. It's a big challenge but one that I am up to."—JANUARY 1990

"ALLAN BORDER TO MERV HUGHES: If you want to sort your control out why don't you look at a place on the pitch just short of a length outside off-stump. MERV TO AB: What for? I never bowl there."

"They should have given me a game two years ago," SAID A SELF-EFFACING MARK WAUGH AFTER HIS CENTURY ON DEBUT AGAINST ENGLAND IN THE 1990-91 SUMMER

"I go home early after the loss. How the (expletive deleted) could we have lost that game today. There is not enough genuine remorse when dismissed because players aren't totally committed to the team. Extremely disappointed with a loss of such kind. We blew it. I am getting very frustrated with the type of team we have become. I am tired of always being the one expected to be putting in. Stuff 'em."—I THROW THE TOYS OUT OF THE COT AFTER WE WERE BEATEN BY 12 RUNS IN A ONE-DAY GAME AGAINST THE WEST INDIES AT THE GABBA, JANUARY 1992

"Everything is a colour
Every success, every failure
All making us strive harder
If you know your dream
Your dedication is complete
And your focus is clear
Anything is possible" —FROM A MOTIVATION TAPE I WATCHED IN FEBRUARY 1990

"Want everything. Stay low, move outside every ball. Wait for the ball and stay down. Block out all else and make others enjoy it."—19 SEP. 1990

"Long game, distracted casual approach by us. Even I allowed myself to entertain thoughts of finishing the tour ... soft (expletive deleted). I was going to ensure it didn't happen."—I LAMENT OUR DROPPED GUARD WHEN WE LOST TO ENGLAND IN THE FINAL TEST OF THE 1993 ASHES SERIES AT THE OVAL

"From those to whom much has been given, much is expected."
—FORMER WIMBLEDON CHAMPION AND TENNIS GREAT ARTHUR ASHE. I DISCOVERED AND NOTED IT IN FEBRUARY 1992

when he passed Sunil Gavaskar's all-time run-making record—I suddenly "broke into goose bumps".

And some things which mean everything to me but not a lot to anyone else like the day after the 1990-91 season when Geoff Marsh said to me, "I reckon you'll win the car for the player of the season." Of course I didn't but it went down in the diaries as "a very touching moment".

The diaries also document key points of madcap celebrations after Test wins—from David Boon falling into a pot plant after a Test win at Old Trafford on the 1993 Ashes tour to Steve Waugh and I, both a fair bit tipsy, posing as each other during a hilarious phone interview with a Melbourne radio station after another victory on the same tour.

On one occasion in my diary an entry was nothing more than an illustration of the Ashes urn which I sketched in pencil. Under it I wrote the words, "Who's it to be?"

It gave me great satisfaction to write another sentence—"It is us."—at the end of the 1990–91 summer.

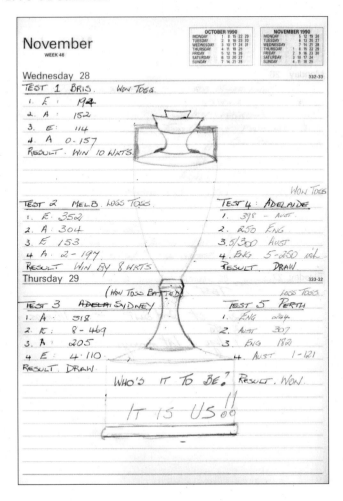

FROM THE HEALY DIARIES

"I score 102, my first Test century. Absolutely stoked, as was Tugga (Steve Waugh). Simmo says he could not have been prouder if I was his son. Warnie, Maysie and Boon ... amazing joy. They say I deserve everything I get. We win Test. Boonie gives me huge wraps all night before falling into pot plant and later falling asleep in toilet having a smoke ... —GREAT DAY IN MY LIFE."

"I am not a four hitter. I am a worker, a chipper. Watch each ball and build my intensity. I have been too impatient and overawed by the situation."—MARCH 1992

"Didn't realise change in field for there were two men back and I hooked in the air straight to backward square. You idiot. Hit them well but not mentally tough enough."—OUT HOOKING, OUTFOXED BY DAVID HOOKES IN A SHEFFIELD SHIELD MATCH AGAINST SOUTH AUSTRALIA, 24 NOVEMBER 1988

"It's not what's in front of you that blocks your way, it's what's inside you that holds you back. Think big."

"Simmo revs us: He said we expect perfection from all around us but do we expect it from ourselves. We are getting a bit arrogant and rude to people."—COACH BOB SIMPSON GIVES THE BOYS AN EXCELLENT ADDRESS ON THE 1993 ASHES TOUR

"Every other superstar was there as well,"—CRAIG MCDERMOTT AFTER THE GOLD COAST INDY BALL IN 1993, WHILE HIS TEAM-MATES WERE CAMPAIGNING IN NEW ZEALAND

"I miss stumping to allow Pakistan to win. My first real blemish for the game. F— IT ... unbelievable feeling. I was numb and couldn't talk for one hour. Finally start with swear words only. Can't believe we lost. Life's realities are experienced from the canvas."—AFTER MISSING THE LAST BALL STUMPING AGAINST PAKISTAN IN KARACHI, SEPTEMBER 1994

"I can smell it on him." "He's wetting his pants." "Show them what us niggers can do." "We know what these people are like." "Get 'em on the step ladder."—WEST INDIAN SLEDGES DIRECTED OUR WAY DURING THE 1991 TOUR THERE

"Let's get him out of the basement and on the top floor." "He wants to hook 'Benji', I think we can help him." "Let's get 10 men on this bus." "Keep him guessing Ambi."—WEST INDIAN SLEDGES FROM THE 1992-93 SERIES IN AUSTRALIA

"Fire and Fear: Fear must be made to work for you ... manipulate it." —MIKE TYSON'S TRAINER GUS D'AMATO (FROM TYSON'S BIOGRAPHY)

"Perfect your skills to almost make them look effortless (not lazy— easy). At the same time don't expect plaudits for your skills which you try to hide."—FEBRUARY 1990

"How f—ing great is this. The plans, the execution, the result. Huge sense of satisfaction. Most complete feeling of my career. Probably because I've been privy to the plans. There's a lot of love in the rooms." —VICTORY OVER THE WEST INDIES, 4 MAY 1995

An emotional moment for the Australian team, Boonie and I share the singing of "Underneath the Southern Cross" after our Test series win over Sri Lanka in Adelaide in 1996.

VIV JENKINS/AUSTRALIAN CRICKET BOARD

Australia has lost two greats in recent times; David Boon announced his retirement from international cricket in 1995-96, Allan Border just a season after becoming the world's leading Test run-getter in Christchurch in 1993.

An era ends—long time coach Bob Simpson talks tactics with me— and another begins— I enjoy a World Series victory celebration with the new coach, then a selector, Geoff Marsh.

The dressing room scene just after we'd beaten Sri Lanka at the SCG to clinch the 1995-96 World Series. It was my first solo effort as song leader after being "passed the baton" by Boonie.

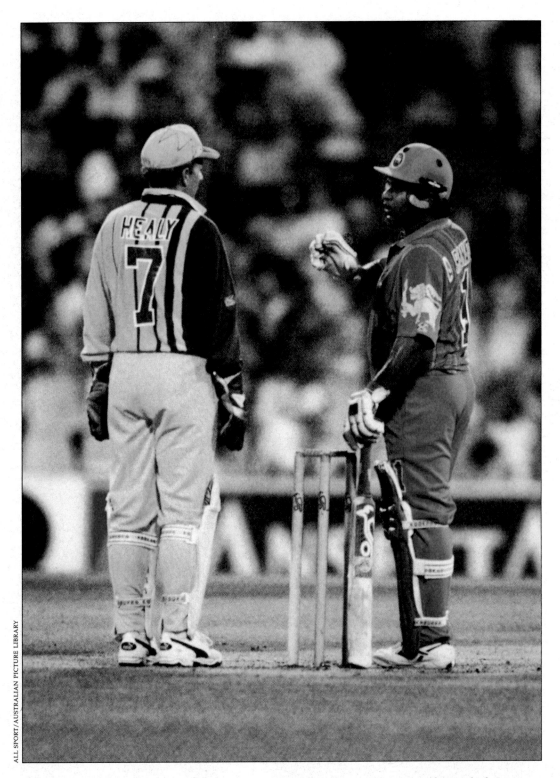

*"OK, 'Porky' ..." Sri Lanka's captain Arjuna Ranatunga makes a point after we had
disagreed on his right to have a runner during the World Series finals.*

Opposite page: *The side of the game that's seldom seen, families. There's a table for eight
when the Taylors and the Healys get together, and when David Boon bid farewell to big
cricket at the Adelaide Oval his wife Pip, in blue, led the standing ovation.*

In Big Mac territory with little Emma.
It was Auckland, 1993, and she'd just turned two.

COURIER-MAIL

Left: *Ever the improviser, Javed Miandad had an impromptu "net" on the concrete in front of the Clem Jones Stand because the practice wickets were too wet.*

Below: *Richard Hadlee. He was a master of the mental side of the game.*

CRAIG SHAW/COURIER-MAIL

I have sometimes been accused of being too self-absorbed in my diaries and must plead guilty to this on at least one occasion. When Helen was waiting to be induced for the birth of our second daughter Laura I was sitting with her in the hospital ward. Hour after hour ticked by, with Helen walking around in a bid to speed up proceedings while I diligently updated my diaries from the South African tour of 1994. As she passed in and out of the ward, Helen said things like, "There are quite a few couples out there," and "It's so nice seeing the husbands and wives walking together." I would nod or say something like, "Yes ... excellent." I was so intent on my diary I didn't even realise she was hoping I might do the same as the other men.

There is one great must when writing a diary—never lie to it. If you do then you might as well throw it out the window. Honesty is simply crucial. If I am making excuses in my diary imagine what I am telling people around me.

There are so many sportsmen who say they are hitting the ball well but everyone around them knows they are batting hopelessly. You can't kid people in sport. Cricket is a big ego thing. No-one likes to be seen as failing or even struggling, but you won't work your way out of it until you admit you are at rock bottom.

I am often super tough on myself, and it once occurred to me that if someone said about me the things I say about myself in the diaries I would never speak to him again. In one entry, after a dreadful shot in a one-day game, I even called for my own sacking, for a lack of pride in my national cap. Once you admit you are struggling you will start to improve.

All sorts of names bob up in my diaries.

The spritely Broncos rugby league hooker Kerrod Walters, with his bold upright and half-cheeky running style, made an impression on me in the early years of the Broncos because he always looked as if he was enjoying the game so much.

I am not sure whether that obvious enjoyment made him play well but it convinced me that, even if you're not playing well, if you look as if you are others around you will play better.

Walters is also a role model for another one of my mental devices, which decrees "Absolute hunger for the game will override negative thoughts."

When I bat in a major match my thought processes are activated by a series of key phrases—one of them is "Greg Matthews". It may surprise some people to learn that the colourful NSW allrounder is a role model for me, but when I was batting with Matthews for Australia I simply marvelled at his ability to not only stay at the wicket but also to squeeze every drop of potential out of the tail.

Sometimes he could put pressure on the tail by playing silly games with them, but he puts so much energy into the other person he often brought out the best in them.

For a bloke with several limitations to his batting, Matthews' record was phenomenal—he scored four Test centuries and averaged 41 though he was chosen as much for his bowling. I feel as if I have more ability with the bat than 'Moey', but my record is vastly inferior to his.

One of the catch phrases I will often write in my diaries is "No outcomes".

There is a tendency in cricket, as in any sport, to be preoccupied with the final outcome and the ramifications of every move. What happens if I drop the next catch? What happens if I get out? What happens if I get an edge?

This type of thought erodes your performance in all sorts of avenues of the game. It is amazing how, if you stop worrying about the outcome of a match, how your performance will improve.

In Guyana on the 1991 West Indian tour my whole goal for the Test was not to worry about the outcome. I was going to do all the hard work and make sure I enjoyed it but the scoreboard would be irrelevant to me. I wasn't going to worry whether we were losing, or in a great position and when I batted I would not worry about getting out.

It was a tough decision to make, because if you are going down in a Test match, as we did there, it is hard not to think about the outcome. But it is amazing how much pressure it takes off you and how it can turn things around and I managed 53 and 47 (run out in both innings) for my best ever Test against the Windies. Those innings and 32 in the final Test of the series at Antigua filled me with confidence and convinced me that was the way you had to play against the Windies.

If all you worried about was the next ball and letting your natural skills take over rather than think "God I hope I don't get a great ball" then you will maximise your chances of success.

THE 1996 WORLD CUP

"Ghandi was gettable ... you blokes will be a piece of cake."

FROM A LETTER TO IAN HEALY JUST BEFORE THE WORLD CUP

It is to the immense relief of most generations of Australian cricketers that their closest association with the term "death threat" came when they watched an action movie or read about violence in some faraway land they never had to visit.

But the sour face of terrorism stalked Australia in the 1995–96 summer as we were preparing for the World Cup in India, Pakistan and Sri Lanka. I received one death threat and another generally abusive letter. It would be easy to dismiss the threat to my life as the work of some off-beat prankster, but it was all the more disturbing for the cool, methodical way in which it was done.

The neatly typed letter was posted from Melbourne and on the back of the envelope was the fictitious name 'Damien Davies'. It appears it was a hoax, but it was unsettling because some of the terminology he used was quite sophisticated. It looked like just another business letter.

The message to me was that the Tamil Tigers had two suicide bombers waiting for Australia to land on the subcontinent during the World Cup—one in Sri Lanka, the other in southern India, in case Australia boycotted Sri Lanka and played all the matches in India, which we ultimately did.

A second abusive letter, mailed from Hobart, was simply titled "Smart arse ... Healy the cheat." It read: "You've never changed. I suppose you will stay at home too. You are like the rest of them, pretty gutless. You live by the sword, you die by the sword. And remember, don't throw sticks at the animals. I loathe the Australian XI."

It was unsigned.

While you can never trivialise death threats, our attitude towards them mellowed slightly when we later spoke to the Indians and Pakistanis during the World Cup.

"What's new? We get them all the time," was their standard line.

The ACB eventually cancelled our trip to Colombo for the opening match of the tournament. That happened after a Colombo bomb blast killed 87 people in March, what you might call the last straw in what had been a summer of unhappy relations between the Sri Lankans and Australians.

The main stumbling block in relations was their captain Arjuna Ranatunga.

Ranatunga is regarded by our side as a world class cricketer and a master of gamesmanship, the most influential person in Sri Lankan cricket whose influence stretches well beyond the boundary of his sport into society.

His father Reggie is Deputy Minister for Transport and Women's Affairs in the Sri Lankan government and one of Arjuna's six brothers, Prasanne, has also embarked on a political career.

The first ripples of concern over the security issue were generated in a low key incident in the first Test in Perth, when Craig McDermott and Ranatunga collided after a McDermott delivery.

Craig believed Ranatunga said after the incident, "You'll take your life in your hands when you visit our country," and he was so upset he reported the statement to match officials, who summoned Ranatunga for an explanation.

Arjuna maintained he had said, "You take your wife in your hands when you visit my country," which seems a strange comment to make during a mid-pitch quarrel.

Later, in Melbourne, Ranatunga made more inflammatory remarks during a net session. He told the press we would cop plenty of abuse when we landed in Colombo for our pre-tour training camp.

And I had a heated run-in with him during the last World Series final in Sydney when he was granted a runner after supposedly being injured.

I said to him, "You can't have a runner for being unfit," to which he shot back "Stay out of this ... shut your mouth." I responded with "Okay, sorry Porky."

He then launched a verbal tirade at me and I ended up receiving a twin-barrelled salvo as Tubsy Taylor told me in a few short sentences to shut up and stay out of it.

That was a fair enough call, but I was aggravated at Arjuna being granted a runner simply for being unfit.

Because we regarded Ranatunga as such as influential figure in Sri Lankan society, we insisted at a meeting with ACB chief executive Graham Halbish that one of the conditions for us to make the World Cup tour would be that Ranatunga state publicly we would be welcome in his country.

But he refused to do so, saying, "I will not dance to the tune of Mr Taylor and Mr Halbish."

I, for one, felt intimidated by the prospect of making the tour. I was feeling quite down on the first morning of our Brisbane training camp, and Simmo asked what the problem was. I told him, "I just don't really want to go. The pressure we are going to cop once we get over there will be too great simply for a cricket tournament."

I am sure I was not the only one feeling that way.

However, our arrival in Calcutta diminished fears; we were wildly greeted by thousands who lined our route to the team motel. And the news from home was tension-relieving as well—Helen told me that when our daughter Emma saw me on the news, she shrieked, "They've speared Daddy!" She had spotted the red mark placed on my head at the airport, the Hindu blessing and welcome.

We beat Kenya in the first match, but lost Craig McDermott for the Cup with a leg strain. I thought Tony Dodemaide, the consistent and underrated Victorian who is a fine one-day bowler, or Jason Gillespie, with his exceptional Sheffield Shield form, had the front-running for the replacement's role. Eventually the nod went to Gillespie.

He was quite a mystery man, so much so that there was indecision in the team about his first name, and Simmo piped up with, "It's Jason ... I've checked."

The standard of our motels in India was generally sound though there was inevitable communication problems with the staff. After a draining day of food poisoning, Michael Slater ordered extra toilet paper to his room at one venue only to be sent a bottle of mineral water.

There were times when room service took some time arriving though, in total contrast, I once had a phone call from a room service waiter asking whether I wanted to order something!

Our second game against India was a tremendous match, in which we galloped out of the gates and looked poised to make around 280 before being restricted to 258 after losing four wickets without scoring a solitary run in the final over.

The player who stood between us and a win was Sachin Tendulkar, India's current batting hero. Australian teams of the early 1980s used to say when Sunil Gavaskar's name came up at team meetings there was often a conspicuous silence. Like Gavaskar, Tendulkar has no obvious soft spot in a beautifully rounded game. Our plan was to bowl just short of a length to him and make him hit on the rise or across the line if he wanted to score runs.

I rate him, Steve Waugh and Brian Lara as the best batsmen in the world. Their methods are very different, yet as for sheer class I can't separate them.

Tendulkar is a very tight technician and has all the strokes as well. Lara is flashier and gives you more of a chance. At times he can be impetuous, for he loves hitting the big fours. Waugh, the ruthless craftsman, simply snuffs out bowling attacks, giving bowlers no chance to get him out, yet scoring at a rate which is more than passable by Test match standards.

You have to go to India to appreciate the pressure that rides with Sachin every innings. His face is simply everywhere in India, advertising everything from jeans to televisions to Pepsi. A King Kong sized photo of Sachin on Bombay's largest advertising hoarding greets tourists on the smog-filled route from the airport to the city and a smaller version of the photo is in most streets.

Glenn McGrath did it beautifully for his first three overs—all maidens—but it all changed because of two shots which were breathtaking illustrations of Sachin's rare and immense talent.

Both were high-risk pull shots which were made to look as if there was no risk at all as they disappeared over the on-side. The first ball wasn't that short but Sachin belted it over midwicket, and the second went squarer but also to the fence.

We turned to Plan B, bowling yorker length. Instead we bowled half volleys and the ball was disappearing to all parts. Suddenly we weren't quite sure what to do. Plan C?

Tendulkar made an exceptional 90 before Mark Waugh slid one past him to give me a prized stumping and we bowled India out for 242 for a 16 run victory.

At our team meeting before our quarter final against New Zealand, the only two players we didn't talk about were Chris Harris and new captain and wicket-keeper Lee Germon. We had talked about fluent left-hander Steve Fleming, and aggressive openers Nathan Astle and Craig Spearman and the dangerous Chris Cairns. Harris, although something of a strokemaking wizard in English league cricket, had a poor record against us, only 85 runs in nine limited overs internationals.

But Harris played brilliantly; from 3–44 they advanced to 3–180 after 30 overs and ended up making an outstanding 8–286.

The key tactical ploy in our innings was sending in a pinch hitter when we lost our second wicket at 84 in the 20th over—Shane Warne.

I floated the suggestion to Michael Slater, not in the team, who agreed with me. But I wasn't going to take it any further, because I had often made similar overtures before and they were knocked back.

I am a supporter of the theory that you need quality batsmen at the end of a one-day innings when the good bowlers come back so you can occasionally get away with sending a big-hitting tailender in during the middle overs, when rival outfits are trying to sneak through their fourth and fifth bowlers.

The move gained momentum when, 15 minutes after I made the suggestion, Steve Waugh came up to me and said, "You know, we should send Warnie in next."

He went and saw Tubby, who endorsed the decision. It proved to be a masterstroke, for Warnie made a hell-raising 24 off 14 balls.

Tugga later showed great courage to hustle a quick 50 despite spraining

*High fives and a hug for Mark Waugh, our man of the moment in the
quarter-final win over New Zealand.*

both ankles in the field—in the dressing room during the change of innings
he had both feet in ice—but Mark Waugh's 110 underpinned the innings.

New Zealand had stacked their side with batsmen and came at us like a
hurricane. But the price for extending their batting line-up was that their
bowling lacked the snap and crackle to keep the pressure on.

We eventually secured victory with 13 balls remaining and I led my first
chant of "Under the Southern Cross". It was an emotional occasion ... the
boys reckoned it was the best ever.

We shared a plane to Chandigarh with the West Indies for the semi-final,
and Brian Lara tried to deceive Shane Warne in flight, so to speak. Lara, via
one of the hostesses, sent a message to Warnie which read: "Hi, my name is
Sushmita Sen. I am a former Miss India and I would love to meet you. I am
sitting in row 22C." Warnie received the letter just before we were due to
land. A quick glance to seat 22C revealed it was indeed occupied by a leggy
customer with big lips. It was no Miss India, but the infamous Curtly Ambrose.

The whitish Chandigarh wicket had an unusually bright sheen about
it, which made it difficult to sight the ball before the batsman got settled.
Mark Waugh was still adjusting his radar when he was a first over victim
to Ambrose, one of those amazing bowlers who never seems to bowl a bad
first over.

TRENT PARKE/NEWS LTD

We sank to 4–15 and just before Michael Bevan went in to bat I asked him how his form was. He said he didn't know because he had hardly hit a ball all tournament. I felt the same way.

Fortunately Bevan and Law put on 138 and I chipped in at the end with 31 to give us a total of 207. It was barely passable, but when you are 4-15 you can't be too fussy.

When the West Indies had advanced to 2–166 at the 41st over, I hadn't given up hope but I had an unusual sort of feeling—I wasn't scared to lose.

The slight thread of hope I was clinging to was that Richie Richardson and Shivnarine Chanderpaul had gone nowhere between the 33rd and 40th over. They were trying to hit the big fours so that victory would come a little easier.

Yet the big fours weren't coming. They were over-hitting or hitting the ball to the field. Nudging the ball around wasn't part of their game plan.

Our one last trump card was that we had saved four of Shane Warne's overs for the last 10 and he took three wickets as the West Indies spiralled out of the tournament.

I ran out Ambrose in the last over when they attempted to run a bye. People might rate it a lucky shot, but I considered it a sweet payback for the 1000 or so times I'd practised the throw in pre-match warm-ups each summer.

The celebrations after that match took me back to the celebrations of Ashes '89 or victory in the West Indies in '95.

The West Indies had become distracted by "the outcome"—they forgot to do the hard work needed to attain it. In the final it happened to Australia.

At 1–134 in the 26th over we were cruising towards a total of 280, yet we made just 7–241. We'd had several hair-raising finishes and now we seemed to be saying to ourselves, "We don't need another tight game, we just want to cruise to a big total, not have to work too hard to defend in the field.

It smacked of us being mentally buggered and the Sri Lankans batted well to make 3–245 off 46.2 overs.

One of my main memories of Cup final day was the distracting way it began. It had rained heavily overnight and there was the expectation of a delayed start. We ended up leaving late, but the match started on time—and when we got there Tubby, who had left earlier to inspect the field said, "Where have you blokes been?" In fact, we'd been told to leave late.

You have to dip your lid to Sri Lanka for their victory in the Cup. One of the greatest achievements any team can make is to change the way the game is played and Sri Lanka has done that.

The way they play seven batsman and go for the doctor from the opening overs will become the norm rather than the exception in future years and cricket can only be the better for it.

Towards the end of the summer it became an increasing irritation to read and hear that we had suddenly become the bad boys of the disputes. This despite the fact that we had not had a player reported all summer, yet Sri Lanka had been involved in ball-tampering and throwing allegations, and vice-captain Aravinda de Silva had belted a dressing room panel in Perth and was involved in a fight with a member at the SCG.

Sri Lanka were painted as the innocents. We gave as good as we got during verbal disputes with the Sri Lankans during the last, highly controversial World Series final in Sydney, but it seemed the blame was not dished out in equal portions.

As Sri Lanka grow in experience and blossom as a Test nation they will lose the sympathy vote that comes with being the underdog. Now that they are world champions at the one-day game they will play under same spotlight that Australia has for many, many years.

Boonie's retirement near the end of the 1995–96 Australian summer surprised me. As you get older as a player three things matter—form, fitness and enthusiasm. They are what I am going to try to maintain over the next few years.

For reasons only known to himself, Boonie was not as enthusiastic throughout the final year of his Test career.

His form to the rest of us seemed okay and if he had picked up his enthusiasm maybe he would have come through it. Maybe, with three kids at home and 11 years of the international grind behind him, he simply had had enough.

His decision to retire followed a tip-off from the selection panel that he was unlikely to be selected in the Australian squads for the tours of Sri Lanka and India which were to follow the 1996 World Cup.

That severely limited his chances of being chosen to play against the West Indies in Australia in 1996–97. If he had played on there was a chance he might get a dreaded tap on the shoulder from the selection panel. Boonie didn't want to take the chance.

After leading the team in an emotional rendition of our war cry, "Under the Southern Cross", he made a small speech passing the tradition over to me. When I joined him on the dressing room table it was a great moment in my career, an honour which simply meant everything to me.

When I got up to do it I was as nervous as if I'd been walking out to bat. My heart was thumping like a drum.

Ian Chappell first learnt the Southern Cross chant when he was playing league cricket in England in the early 1960s. A mate of his used to occasionally sing it from table tops of London bars whenever he was in a nostalgic mood. Ian was told the verse was handed down from a Banjo Paterson poem, but I have not been able to find it.

Another turn of the screw in the semifinal—Warnie gets Ian Bishop.

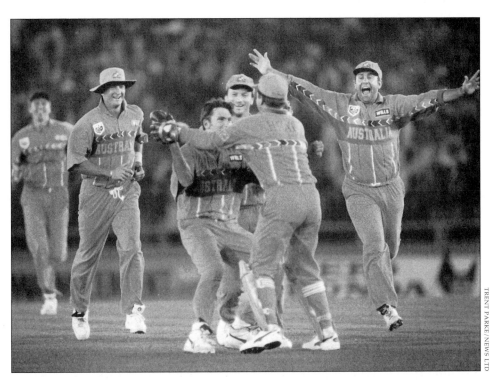

There were no moths under the lights at Chandigarh when Damien Fleming bowled Courtney Walsh to win the semifinal against the West Indies—otherwise captain Mark Taylor would have swallowed one! His joy was understandable—we came back from the dead.

THE VICE-CAPTAINCY

"The Australian cricket vice-captain is more import than Australia's deputy Prime Minister."

OFFBEAT FAX FROM A FAN TO IAN HEALY

I'm not much of a punter but reading the sport pages on a winter morning in 1995 I spotted what I thought was a good thing. It wasn't at Rosehill or Randwick, in fact it wasn't even a horse ... it was me.

Australia was about to choose its next cricket captain and vice-captain and the tipsters' favourites were Mark Taylor as captain and Steve Waugh as his deputy—a New South Wales quinella.

In the minor placings were yours truly and David Boon, the outsider.

I think everyone expected long-time vice-captain Taylor to be the natural choice as captain, but I had a feeling I would be his deputy. I based that on the liberal way Australian cricket likes to spread its power base.

Most of the selectors come from different States, the Board representation is widely, if not quite evenly, spread and the Board chairmanship is also rotated on a three year basis between the states.

Given the pains Australian cricket has gone to give itself an equitable look it would have surprised me if it then appointed a coach (Bob Simpson), captain (Taylor) and vice-captain (Waugh) from the same State ... New South Wales.

On the strength of that hunch I rang Centrebet in Alice Springs to check the odds for a Taylor-Healy quinella. I felt even money would have been a fair quote but when they nominated 4–1, I couldn't get on quickly enough.

The funny thing was that when I rang I told them who I was, but once I had assured them I didn't have any inside oil, they let me on.

I had $200 on and later rang my brothers and sister who also got on.

Later that night I received the call from Melbourne that Tubsy and I would be Australia's new leaders. I had the job—and the Healy family had the bikkies, a slightly bizarre betting plunge.

Earlier the leading foursome Taylor, Boon, Waugh and myself had met with the directors of the Australian Cricket Board. It was regrettable that the Board had to familiarise themselves with the players before making the decision. I hadn't met half the Board members and I can only think their opinion of us would have been shaped by what they had seen of us on television or read in the papers. But given the length of time we had been playing for Australia we should have been more familiar with each other.

I am pleased to say that since those meetings the Board have regularly consulted the players on major matters and the lines of communication are smoother than they used to be.

If I had been offered the captaincy I would have taken it and enjoyed it. But, in the current team structure I believe Taylor was the better choice for the job.

Vice-captain is the position that suits me perfectly, so much so that if Taylor was injured for any length of time I would have to consider whether it would be more beneficial for the team to promote Steve Waugh to the leadership role and leave me as the deputy.

I can handle the Queensland captaincy without a problem, but the Bulls have no Shane Warne.

'Keeping to Warne is my single most important and challenging function in the team and anything that threatens to reduce my efficiency to Shane could not be good for the team. 'Keeping to Warne requires optimum concentra-

Okay, you're now the vice-captain of Australia and you're facing your first media interview, and the first question is a hot one: "Desmond Haynes thinks you're a thief, what do you say about that?" The Cricket Board organised the grilling to prepare me for any potholes in the road ahead.

tion and enormous effort. I often wonder how I would perform at post-match press conferences after a long day over the pegs.

If you have candidates of equal ability, the shrewd move is to give the job to the man with less on his plate. That meant Taylor being the top banana and it could well mean Stephen taking his place.

The vice-captaincy has brought about a necessary change in me. I was now a senior role model in the side and had to behave accordingly, although I did it somewhat reluctantly; one of the themes of my life is to be myself no matter what my role or environment. There is no doubt that whatever larrikin streak lies in me can come rushing to the boil during a celebratory or commiseratory drink.

My wife Helen got it right when she said that if I ever suffer a big fall in life it would be self-induced—my mouth will be the culprit.

Even before the vice-captaincy came my way two unfortunate incidents had moved me to tone down my on-tour let-downs.

After a landslide Test win against England in Melbourne in the 1994–95 summer I was celebrating at the Parkroyal Hotel, still dressed in my playing shirt and baggy green at 5pm, more than four hours after the game had finished.

A group of Englishmen came into the bar and one raised my ire by saying "You blokes think you are pretty good but you have only beaten England."

I leapt onto the front foot with "Yeah, that's right, they are soft and don't care enough for their country and you are probably the same."

His wife reported me to the concierge, who contacted team manager Ian McDonald and the police. 'Macca' demanded I apologise, which I was happy to do, then I headed upstairs to prepare for dinner.

As we emerged from the lifts in the foyer, on the way to dinner, we noticed a policeman. Helen quipped, "Here he is, officer ... you might like to take him away." And to our astonishment, and discomfort, he was actually there to see me.

An incident in Perth at the end of that Ashes-winning series was more unfortunate. I was returning to the team motel late and I encountered two drunken, verbally aggressive English supporters.

I initially tried to appease them by asking them what their problem was, but I gave up and as I started walking away, said, "You're a bunch of losers." Wrong! One of them headbutted me and I ended up in hospital.

I wrote in my diary: "My behaviour when drinking has been too confrontational when people are sledging me or the team. I will either get myself into trouble properly, upset people, or get badly hurt even if I am bullet proof! I must make an effort to curb this behaviour because it is no longer appropriate to my team role and profile. Improve this as of now ... I am no longer a normal person."

PHIL NORRISH / COURIER-MAIL

*It's not as serious as it looks. I was participating in a promotion
for "Crimestoppers" in Queensland.*

So I have become more mellow and careful, but it's a delicate balancing act, trying not to change too drastically because I staunchly defend the benefits of a full-hearted celebration or wake after a Test.

There's not too many times when a captain is stumped and has to turn to the vice-captain for support. It's mainly in the bad times that my opinion is sought and when I see Tubsy walking over I tend to think, "Oh no, here we go ..."

However, I see a very definite role for the vice-captain and one which has been down-played in Australian cricket over the years because we have had such dominant captains from Sir Donald Bradman through to Ian and Greg Chappell.

Under the strong, long-serving leadership of these men there was probably not a great scope for the role of a deputy but in an era when we play so regularly and the demands of the media and world touring are so great the second man can be used as a pressure release.

Geoff Marsh shaped my thinking on this because I admired the way, particularly in the later stages of his career, he took pressure off AB. 'Swampy' was quite good at picking when a player was down or not quite with it and he was able to pep them up.

When the captain and vice-captain are close in experience—as Taylor and I are—they can work together to share the load and ease the burden.

If some-one has a gripe in the team, I can go to them as vice-captain and try to sort it out. The Australian side should not have to wait for the captain to be the mediator in every team issue, particularly when he has so many major matters to attend to.

There may be occasions when the captain has a word to one of the players who is having problems and for the next week or so, while the captain is occupied with the bigger picture, I and other senior players will be keeping an eye on that player.

As I prattle on about team dynamics and my new role it has struck me how my world has changed over the past eight years.

Suddenly the memory of one bewildering April Fool's Day, when a suspicious rookie edged cautiously into the spotlight, seems a life-time away.